RAND Program Evaluation Toolkit for
COUNTERING VIOLENT EXTREMISM

Todd C. Helmus, Miriam Matthews,
Rajeev Ramchand, Sina Beaghley, David Stebbins,
Amanda Kadlec, Michael A. Brown,
Aaron Kofner, Joie D. Acosta

Prepared for the Department of Homeland Security
Approved for public release; distribution unlimited

For more information on this publication, visit www.rand.org/t/TL243

Library of Congress Cataloging-in-Publication Data is available for this publication.
ISBN: 978-0-8330-9724-8

Published by the RAND Corporation, Santa Monica, Calif.
© Copyright 2017 RAND Corporation
RAND® is a registered trademark.

Cover images: Albany Associates/Flickr (top); hxdbzxy/GettyImages (middle);
teekid/GettyImages (bottom).

Limited Print and Electronic Distribution Rights

This document and trademark(s) contained herein are protected by law. This representation of RAND intellectual property is provided for noncommercial use only. Unauthorized posting of this publication online is prohibited. Permission is given to duplicate this document for personal use only, as long as it is unaltered and complete. Permission is required from RAND to reproduce, or reuse in another form, any of its research documents for commercial use. For information on reprint and linking permissions, please visit www.rand.org/pubs/permissions.

The RAND Corporation is a research organization that develops solutions to public policy challenges to help make communities throughout the world safer and more secure, healthier and more prosperous. RAND is nonprofit, nonpartisan, and committed to the public interest.

RAND's publications do not necessarily reflect the opinions of its research clients and sponsors.

Support RAND
Make a tax-deductible charitable contribution at
www.rand.org/giving/contribute

www.rand.org

Preface

Violent extremism poses a threat to the lives of those living in the United States and abroad. Extremist individuals and groups embrace a variety of motivations and methods, and their chosen targets may be equally varied. Those who perpetuate such acts may be motivated by an ideology (such as extremist religious beliefs), a specific issue (such as animal liberation), or a separatist/political cause.[1] Community-based organizations with the goal of countering violent extremism (CVE) similarly vary in their focus and activities. Such organizations may lead discussion groups or seminars, develop information campaigns, or hold youth sporting events. They may address extremism by refuting narratives from those seeking to radicalize others, by promoting cultural competency or awareness, or by fostering supportive climates and promoting positive social bonds.

Regardless of the approaches these programs take or whether they even identify as CVE programs, evaluations are critical for assessing the impact of their activities and can be used as the basis for decisions about whether to sustain, modify, or scale up existing efforts. The U.S. Department of Homeland Security's Office of Community Partnerships asked the RAND Corporation to create a toolkit to guide future evaluations of community-based CVE programs. The overall goal of the toolkit is to help those responsible for CVE programs determine whether their programs produce beneficial effects, to identify areas for improvement, and, ultimately, to guide the responsible allocation of scarce resources.

This toolkit is based on RAND's Getting To Outcomes® (GTO) approach, an evidence-based model designed to help community-based programs conduct self-evaluations. We specifically adapted this toolkit from the RAND Suicide Prevention Program Evaluation Toolkit, published in 2013 and available online at www.rand.org/t/TL111. The GTO approach, and its application to the assessment of suicide prevention programs, provided an excellent foundation for this toolkit. First, like violent extremism, suicide is a very rare event that involves both thought (motivation) and action (violence). Programs that work to prevent suicide, like those that aim to prevent violent extremism, are challenged to produce evidence that the program has actually prevented suicides (or, in this case, extremist acts). Thus, these toolkits recommend the use of proximal outcomes for both types of programs. To adapt the Suicide Prevention Toolkit to address CVE programming, RAND researchers examined the peer-reviewed

---

[1] According to the White House *Strategic Implementation Plan for Empowering Local Partners to Prevent Violent Extremism in the United States*, the phrase *countering violent extremism* (CVE) refers to "proactive actions to counter efforts by extremists to recruit, radicalize, and mobilize followers to violence." These proactive actions seek to address the conditions and reduce the underlying factors that give rise to radicalization and recruitment (Executive Office of the President, 2016, p. 2).

RAND Program Evaluation Toolkit for Countering Violent Extremism

literature and other evaluation toolkits and elicited feedback from program staff responsible for implementing CVE programs.

The contents of this toolkit will be of particular interest to managers and directors of community-based CVE programs, as well as program funders. Although the toolkit is tailored to the needs of evaluators with limited prior experience, the contents may also be of interest to academic program evaluation experts who assist programs with evaluations or conduct studies of program effectiveness.

A companion document, *Development and Pilot Test of the RAND Program Evaluation Toolkit for Countering Violent Extremism*, provides additional background on the toolkit's development and refinement and is available online at www.rand.org/t/RR1799.

This research was sponsored by the Office of Community Partnerships in the U.S. Department of Homeland Security and conducted in the International Security and Defense Policy Center of the RAND National Defense Research Institute, a federally funded research and development center sponsored by the Office of the Secretary of Defense, the Joint Staff, the Unified Combatant Commands, the Navy, the Marine Corps, the defense agencies, and the defense Intelligence Community.

For more information on the RAND International Security and Defense Policy Center, see www.rand.org/nsrd/ndri/centers/isdp or contact the director (contact information is provided on the web page).

RAND Program Evaluation Toolkit for Countering Violent Extremism

Contents

Preface iii
Tools vii
Figures ix

CHAPTER ONE

Introduction and Overview 1

Intended Audience 1
Toolkit Goals and Specific Aims 2
Evaluation Challenges Addressed 2
How the Toolkit Was Developed 3
User's Guide 3
Start Using the Toolkit 4
Summary 6

CHAPTER TWO

Identify Your Program's Core Components for Evaluation and Build a Logic Model 7

Specify Core Components 7
Use Core Components to Build a Logic Model 34
Assess the Quality of Your Program's Logic Model 37
Summary 42

CHAPTER THREE

Design an Evaluation for Your Program 43

Learn the Types of Evaluation Designs 43
Identify Issues Pertinent to Your Evaluation Design 44
Select an Evaluation Design 51
Assess the Quality of the Design 53
Summary 53

RAND Program Evaluation Toolkit for Countering Violent Extremism

CHAPTER FOUR

Select Evaluation Measures for Your Program 55

Select Process Evaluation Measures 55
Select Outcome Evaluation Measures 58
Assess the Quality of Selected Measures 64
Summary 65

CHAPTER FIVE

Use Evaluation Data to Improve Your Program 67

Assess Participation in Your Evaluation 67
Interpret the Evaluation Data 70
Make a Plan to Improve Your Program 74
Conclusion 79

APPENDIX A

Creating Your Own Survey 81

APPENDIX B

Social Media Metrics 99

APPENDIX C

Analyze Your Program's Evaluation Data 105

Glossary of Terms 131

References 133

Tools

Worksheets

2.1.	Identifying Core Components	9
3.1.	Issues to Consider for My Program	49
5.1.	Assessing Participation in Your Program's Evaluation	69
5.2.	Review Program Outcomes, with Example	71
5.3.	Review Program Outcomes	72
5.4.	Program Improvement Plan	78
A.1.	Steps for Creating an Assessment Survey	89

Templates

2.1.	Blank Program Logic Model Template	35
2.2.	Sample Program Logic Model	36
3.1.	Evaluation Planner	52

Checklists

1.1.	Is This Toolkit Right for My Program?	5
2.1.	Is Your Logic Model Complete and Appropriately Detailed?	38
2.2.	Are the Core Components of Your Logic Model Appropriately Aligned?	39
3.1.	Does Your Evaluation Plan Consider the Following Factors?	53
4.1.	To What Extent Do the Measures Selected Align with Your Program's Target Population, Activities, and Outcomes?	65
5.1.	What CQI Actions Are Needed to Improve the Program?	76

vii

Tables

3.1.	Types of Evaluation Designs	45
4.1.	Sample Process Measures	57
4.2.	Sample Outcome Measures for CVE Programs Addressing Individuals at Risk for Violent Extremism	59
4.3.	Sample Outcome Measures for CVE Programs Addressing Communities That Influence Individuals at Risk for Violent Extremism	62
5.1.	Results-Based Scenarios and Associated Strategies for Program Improvement	75
A.1.	Use Simple Words and Phrases	83
C.1.	Types of Analyses Addressed in Each Data Analysis Primer	110

Figures

2.1.	Objectives for Broad Audiences of CVE Programs	18
2.2.	Examples of CVE Program Outputs	24
C.1.	Sample Attendance Sheet with Unique Identifiers	107
C.2.	Survey Cover Sheet with Unique Identifier	107
C.3.	Formatting Ranges in Excel	108

Chapter One: Introduction and Overview

Chapter One
Introduction and Overview

Objective:

To explain the toolkit's purpose and content and to help you decide whether this toolkit is appropriate for use with your program.

Evaluations can provide valuable information to guide program development, implementation, and modification. This toolkit is designed to assist with program evaluation. In this chapter, we review the intended audience for this toolkit, the toolkit's goals and specific aims, and the evaluation challenges that the toolkit addresses. We conclude with a brief user's guide that previews the toolkit's content and offers tips for its use and navigation.

Intended Audience

This toolkit is designed to be used by community-based organizations that are implementing programs to counter violent extremism (referred to as CVE programs throughout this toolkit). As mentioned in the preface, these types of programs vary considerably. As you will read in Chapter Two, these programs may address extremism directly or indirectly, such as by promoting cultural awareness and acceptance or bolstering social bonds within communities. They can pursue these goals through structured and unstructured activities, including blog posts on websites, films, and seminars or workshops. CVE programs may seek to counter a variety of different types of extremism, including religious and right- or left-wing extremism, or they may seek to counter violence without much thought to extremist motivations. City, state, and federal agencies that fund or otherwise support CVE programming may encourage associated community organizations to use this toolkit. In addition, those responsible for assessing or evaluating CVE programs may be interested in the contents of this toolkit.

RAND Program Evaluation Toolkit for Countering Violent Extremism

Toolkit Goals and Specific Aims

The overall goals of this toolkit are to help those responsible for CVE programs determine whether their programs produce beneficial effects, to improve program performance, and, ultimately, to guide the responsible allocation of scarce resources. To accomplish these goals, this toolkit aims to

1. Help you design an evaluation that is based on your type of program and available resources and expertise.
2. Support the selection of measures for new evaluations and augment or enhance ongoing evaluations.
3. Offer basic guidance on how to analyze evaluation data and then use these data to improve the effectiveness of CVE programs.

Each chapter of the toolkit contributes to these aims, which can be achieved by working through the entire toolkit. To design an evaluation for your program, you will need to first identify your program's core components (**Chapter Two**). You will then need to weigh the benefits and costs of specific evaluation designs so that you can select a design that is appropriate for your program's resources and expertise (**Chapter Three**). Finally, you will select your evaluation measures (**Chapter Four**). Sample measures are included in Chapter Four. **Chapter Five** offers guidance on using evaluation results for program improvement, while the appendixes provide technical guidance on data collection and analysis.

Evaluation Challenges Addressed

Evaluating CVE programs has been a challenge for many program staff. This toolkit will help address two common challenges to evaluating these types of programs.

Challenge 1: Violent extremism is a relatively rare event, so it is difficult to use reductions in terrorist attacks or decreases in the number of "violent extremists" as outcomes for CVE programming.

The toolkit provides options for evaluating intermediate outcomes that, in theory, will reduce the risk of terrorist attacks or the probability that a program's target audience will support violent extremism or act on violent extremist views.

Challenge 2: Many programs have multiple components, making it difficult to discern the components or characteristics that are responsible for any observed effect.

The toolkit supports the development of a program logic model—a graphical depiction of the rationale and expectations of a program that ties specific program activities to specific intermediate outcomes. In Chapter Two, we guide readers through the steps needed to create a logic model. This helps programs better identify specific program goals and methods. By creating a logic model and connecting it to evaluation approaches and methods, the toolkit helps users apply the most appropriate evaluation methods.

Chapter One: Introduction and Overview

How the Toolkit Was Developed

This toolkit was adapted from the RAND Suicide Prevention Program Evaluation Toolkit (Acosta et al., 2013). Specifically, Chapters One, Three, and Five were largely replicated from the Suicide Prevention Toolkit, but Chapters Two and Four needed to be tailored to CVE programs, and we added technical guidance for these programs, which can be found the toolkit's appendix matter. To tailor the toolkit to CVE programs, we interviewed 30 CVE program managers across the United States and conducted a systematic review of the CVE program evaluation literature, including evaluation studies. In Chapter Two, we encourage readers to create a logic model and guide them through the steps to do so; our interviews with CVE program managers helped us tailor the logic model to U.S.-based CVE programs. We also used the literature review to identify the types of evaluation approaches and measures that have been used elsewhere. More information about how the toolkit was developed can be found in a companion report (Beaghley et al., 2017).

The Getting To Outcomes® Approach

Like the RAND Suicide Prevention Evaluation Toolkit, this toolkit is based on the Getting To Outcomes® (GTO) approach. GTO is the only evidence-based model and intervention proven to increase programs' ability to conduct self-evaluations (see Acosta and Chinman, 2011; Chinman et al., 2012, 2013). GTO was developed with support from the Centers for Disease Control and Prevention and the Substance Abuse and Mental Health Services Administration to help communities plan, implement, and evaluate the impact of programs that work to prevent negative behaviors among adolescents (e.g., drug use, underage drinking). The ten-step model describes the activities required to obtain positive results from any prevention program. For more information on GTO, visit www.rand.org/health/projects/getting-to-outcomes.

User's Guide

Overview of Content

The remainder of this toolkit walks users through a series of worksheets and checklists. These worksheets and checklists will help you create a detailed and complete logic model that serves as the foundation for your program's evaluation design (**Chapter Two**) and a plan for your program's evaluation (**Chapter Three**). The evaluation plan will also specify the process and outcome measures that can be used to evaluate your program (**Chapter Four**). In **Chapter Five**, we help you interpret the findings so that they can be used for continuous quality improvement.

The appendixes contain technical instructions on data collection and analysis. We have also included a glossary of some of the less familiar terms we use in this toolkit.

A detailed description of how the toolkit was developed is available in the companion report (Beaghley et al., 2017).

RAND Program Evaluation Toolkit for Countering Violent Extremism

Potential Benefits

This toolkit will help you achieve the following objectives:

- Identify your program's core components and use them to develop a complete and detailed logic model that summarizes your program.
- Focus on available resources and important needs in your community.
- Collect and apply evaluation data to improve the implementation and effectiveness of your program.

The toolkit is designed to guide users through a series of sequential steps in designing and implementing a program evaluation. Repeating the process on a regular basis will help you continually improve your CVE program and will help the program achieve its intended outcomes, which can ultimately result in fewer violent extremists in your community.

Tips for Navigating the Toolkit

This document contains several types of tools, which are marked with corresponding signposts. Worksheets are also available electronically at http://www.rand.org/pubs/tools/TL243.html.

Worksheets

- Ask you to answer key questions

Checklists

- Help direct you through the toolkit
- Provide guidelines to review your own work

Templates

- Blank forms for use in planning
- Complete planning forms to use as an example

Tables

- Summarize relevant research

Start Using the Toolkit

Checklist 1.1 will help you decide whether this toolkit is appropriate for your CVE program. If the toolkit is right for you, it is time to start using it! Be sure to use the toolkit sequentially—proceeding from Chapter Two to Chapter Three, from Chapter Three to Chapter Four, and so on. Worksheets are intended to inform other worksheets in later sections of the toolkit. Starting in the middle of the toolkit may require referring back to earlier chapters. Therefore, we strongly encourage users to go through the toolkit sequentially.

Chapter One: Introduction and Overview

Checklist 1.1
Is This Toolkit Right for My Program?

1. Are you planning to implement a CVE program, or are you currently implementing a CVE program?

☐ Yes ⟶ This toolkit is right for you!

☐ No ⟶ This toolkit is intended primarily for individuals who are currently implementing or planning to implement an CVE program or who have selected a specific CVE program to implement.

2. Are you interested in beginning an evaluation of your CVE program or enhancing your existing evaluation efforts?

☐ Yes ⟶ This toolkit is right for you!

☐ No ⟶ Proceed to Question 3.

3. Are you looking for evaluation measures for your CVE program?

☐ Yes ⟶ This toolkit is right for you! Evaluation measures are available in **Chapter Four**. However, we strongly recommend working through the toolkit sequentially.

☐ No ⟶ Proceed to Question 4.

4. Have you already collected evaluation data on your CVE program that you need help analyzing?

☐ Yes ⟶ This toolkit is right for you! Guidance on evaluation data analysis is provided in Appendix C.

☐ No ⟶ Proceed to Question 5.

5. Do you need help interpreting evaluation data that you have already collected or applying evaluation data to improve your program?

☐ Yes ⟶ This toolkit is right for you! Guidance on interpreting evaluation data is available in Chapter Five. However, we strongly recommend working through the toolkit sequentially.

☐ No ⟶ Proceed to Question 6.

RAND Program Evaluation Toolkit for Countering Violent Extremism

Checklist 1.1
Is This Toolkit Right for My Program?

6. Are you interested in structuring the relationship among your resources, activities, and outcomes into a logic model for your CVE program?[1]

☐ Yes ⟶ This toolkit is right for you!

☐ No ⟶ It is likely that the types of information provided in this toolkit are not applicable to your CVE program.

Summary

This chapter described the purpose and content in the toolkit to help you decide whether this toolkit is appropriate for use with your program and provided a brief summary of how the toolkit was developed. Now that you have read this chapter and completed **Checklist 1.1**, you should know whether this toolkit is right for you and your CVE program. If it is, proceed to **Chapter Two**, which will help you identify the core components of your CVE program and develop a logic model for your program that can be used to guide your evaluation design.

---

[1] Again, a logic model is a graphical depiction of the rationale and expectations of a program (Leviton et al., 2010). A logic model clarifies the causal relationships among program resources, activities, and outcomes (McLaughlin and Jordan, 1999; Wholey, Hatry, and Newcomer, 2010).

Chapter Two: Core Components and Logic Model

Objective:

To provide guidance on how to develop a logic model that will be used in subsequent chapters to plan your program evaluation.

Chapter Two

Identify Your Program's Core Components for Evaluation and Build a Logic Model

In this chapter, we will help you identify the core components of your CVE program by considering the available resources, target audience, program activities and their corresponding objectives, intended outcomes, and community needs being met. Then, we will help you organize these elements into a logic model to clearly visualize the relationships and dependencies between components. Finally, we will help you review the logic model, assessing whether it is complete and reasonable.

Specify Core Components

Reason for Assessing Core Components
To conduct an effective evaluation of your CVE program, it is important to have a clear understanding of the components that make up the program, as well as the interplay between these elements.

How to Assess Core Components
Your CVE program's core components are the resources available to the program; the activities and program objectives, target population, and intended outcomes of the program; any current evaluation activities being conducted; and the need being addressed by the program. Ensuring that these components are well specified will facilitate the development of your evaluation plan.

As stated in Chapter One, one of the challenges with evaluating CVE programs is that they often have multiple components. When assessing program components, it's best to think through each component or activ-

7

RAND Program Evaluation Toolkit for Countering Violent Extremism

ity. For example, if you have two activities, go through the toolkit for the first activity, then go through it again for the second activity. If a single activity has different intended outcomes for different audiences (e.g., a video may serve a different purpose when shown to law enforcement personnel than it does for those at risk of becoming violent extremists), work through the core components separately for each audience. Your program may ultimately have many different logic models that will help guide your evaluations.

In **Worksheet 2.1**, we provide guidance to help you identify the core components of your CVE program. Where possible, we have included categories derived from the core components of typical CVE programs. However, these categories are not necessarily exhaustive; if you do not believe that your core components fit into a preestablished category, use the "Other" space provided to identify the core components that are unique to your program.

Chapter Two: Core Components and Logic Model

Worksheet 2.1
Identifying Core Components

Fill in responses to each of the questions below to help build your program's logic model.

Resources

Resources are the investments, or "inputs," for the program. The performance of program activities and the fulfillment of program goals depend on these resources. A successful program needs adequate resources to fill program needs, as well as prudent allocation of these resources to avoid wasting time and money. Below is a list of the most common resources.

1. Specify which of these resources are available to the program:

☐ Physical space

Describe:

_____
_____
_____
_____
_____
_____
_____

☐ Staff (including their expertise and availability)

Describe:

_____
_____
_____
_____
_____
_____
_____

RAND Program Evaluation Toolkit for Countering Violent Extremism

Worksheet 2.1
Identifying Core Components

☐ Materials or technologies (e.g., videos, DVD players, computers)

Describe:

_____
_____
_____
_____
_____
_____
_____
_____
_____

☐ Funding

Describe:

_____
_____
_____
_____
_____
_____
_____
_____
_____

☐ Other

Describe:

_____
_____
_____
_____
_____
_____
_____
_____
_____

Chapter Two: Core Components and Logic Model

Worksheet 2.1
Identifying Core Components

Next, we'll need to transform these descriptions into well-specified bullets that describe program resources. Below are examples of well-specified and poorly specified lists of resources.

Poorly Specified Examples	Well-Specified Examples
• Intervention staff	• One full-time-equivalent staff member who organizes, schedules, and delivers workshops • A large volunteer base from the community that can be leveraged as needed
• Money	• $50,000 funding to cover 1.5 full-time-equivalent program staff
• Equipment needed to run the program	• Donated space for program activities at the local community center • Presentation materials (e.g., laptop, easel)
• Relationships with key partners	• A memorandum of understanding with the school district to conduct trainings at each school once per year

Describe these resources using a list of well-specified bullet points:

_____
_____
_____
_____
_____
_____
_____
_____
_____
_____

RAND Program Evaluation Toolkit for Countering Violent Extremism

Worksheet 2.1
Identifying Core Components

Program's Target Population

The *target population* is the group intended to benefit from the program. For CVE programs, there are two broad categories into which most target audiences can be grouped: (1) individuals at risk of violent extremism and (2) the broader community that surrounds and potentially influences those at risk of violent extremism. An example of at-risk individuals might be disaffected youth. Examples of the broader community can be family members, religious leaders, and other influential community leaders, such as law enforcement and federal, state, and local government officials.

2. Before identifying whether your program targets individuals at risk or the broader community, specify the demographic characteristics of the audience that your CVE program targets:

☐ Age groups (e.g., adolescents, the elderly)

Describe:

_____
_____
_____
_____
_____
_____

☐ Genders

Describe:

_____
_____
_____
_____
_____
_____

Chapter Two: Core Components and Logic Model

Worksheet 2.1
Identifying Core Components

☐ Community, race, ethnicity, religion, or country of origin

Describe:

_____
_____
_____
_____
_____
_____
_____

☐ Professions

Describe:

_____
_____
_____
_____
_____
_____
_____

☐ Region or online community (e.g., residents of Los Angeles County, Facebook users who click on your organization's banner ad)

Describe:

_____
_____
_____
_____
_____
_____
_____

RAND Program Evaluation Toolkit for Countering Violent Extremism

**Worksheet 2.1
Identifying Core Components**

☐ People with certain characteristics (e.g., high school dropouts)

Describe:

_____
_____
_____
_____
_____
_____
_____
_____
_____

☐ Other

Describe:

_____
_____
_____
_____
_____
_____
_____
_____
_____

Now, looking over the target audiences you described above, determine whether your program targets individuals at risk for violent extremism, communities that influence individuals at risk for violent extremism, or both. Identify and describe your target audience(s) below using well-specified bullet points (e.g., rather than "high school students," a well specified example might be "14- to 18-year-old students in all Minneapolis public schools").

Chapter Two: Core Components and Logic Model

**Worksheet 2.1
Identifying Core Components**

Use well-specified bullet points to describe target audiences:

☐ Individuals at risk for violent extremism

Describe:

_____
_____
_____
_____
_____
_____
_____
_____
_____

☐ Communities that influence individuals at risk for violent extremism

Describe:

_____
_____
_____
_____
_____
_____
_____
_____
_____

If you checked both of the above boxes, try to determine whether each target audience merits its own evaluation. Many programs employ multiple different interventions to reach different target audiences. For example, the same program might train parents and religious leaders to detect and intervene in youth radicalization *and* use information campaigns to sway at-risk youth away from extremism. In this case, each of these interventions would represent a unique "program" in need of evaluation.

RAND Program Evaluation Toolkit for Countering Violent Extremism

Worksheet 2.1
Identifying Core Components

Program's Activities and Objectives

Activities are actions and efforts that make up the program and are employed to reach the program's goals. Activities include the tools, services, and products that the program provides to its target audience. Most CVE programs engage in one of four program activities: communication (publishing or publicizing information), training/education, counseling, or group activities (e.g., performing arts or sports groups). Some activities (e.g., counseling) may be target specific audiences (e.g,, individuals at risk of violent extremism).

3. Specify which of these activities the program engages in:

☐ Communication (e.g., films, posters, blog posts, social media messages)

Describe:

_____
_____
_____
_____
_____
_____
_____

☐ Training/education (e.g., workshops)

Describe:

_____
_____
_____
_____
_____
_____
_____
_____

Chapter Two: Core Components and Logic Model

**Worksheet 2.1
Identifying Core Components**

☐ Counseling (e.g., mental health or spiritual)
Describe:
_____
_____
_____
_____
_____
_____
_____
_____

☐ Group activities (e.g., sports or social clubs, after-school programs, Boy Scouts/Girl Scouts)
Describe:
_____
_____
_____
_____
_____
_____
_____
_____

☐ Other
Describe:
_____
_____
_____
_____
_____
_____
_____
_____

RAND Program Evaluation Toolkit for Countering Violent Extremism

Worksheet 2.1
Identifying Core Components

Objectives are the goals or intended outcomes that your program seeks to engender. For example, your program may seek to alter participants' core beliefs about radicalization, or it may seek to educate parents on the causes and symptoms of extremism. **Figure 2.1** lists several example program objectives that differ according to the two primary target audiences described above.

Figure 2.1
Objectives for Broad Audiences of CVE Programs

Objectives of interest for individuals at risk	• Counter violent extremist opinions and ideologies • Improve psychological health, address moral concerns • Enhance positive social networks • Reduce political grievances • Improve social/economic integration
Objectives of interest for community or community members	• Help community members understand and identify violent extremism and risks • Build the capacity of community members to identify/engage with at-risk individuals • Build the capacity of positive and influential members or leaders of the community to credibly counter violent extremist ideologies • Create environments that are accepting of minority groups • Promote policies that address political grievances • Strengthen government capacity to curtail violent extremism

4. Specify the objectives that your program seeks to achieve:

Objectives for CVE programs targeting individuals at risk for violent extremism

☐ Counter violent extremist opinions and ideology (e.g., help participants refute extremist narratives, promote tolerance and other values antithetical to extremism, discredit extremist organizations).

Describe:

_____
_____
_____
_____
_____

Chapter Two: Core Components and Logic Model

**Worksheet 2.1
Identifying Core Components**

☐ Improve psychological issues and/or address moral concerns (e.g., reduce mental illness, enhance psychological functioning).

Describe:

_____
_____
_____
_____
_____

☐ Enhance positive social networks (e.g., build strong social networks to prevent alienation and isolation).

Describe:

_____
_____
_____
_____
_____

☐ Reduce political grievances (e.g., promote engagements or dialogue between government representatives and at-risk communities).

Describe:

_____
_____
_____
_____
_____

RAND Program Evaluation Toolkit for Countering Violent Extremism

Worksheet 2.1
Identifying Core Components

☐ Improve social/economic integration (e.g., improve target audience economic conditions and enhance social or economic integration).

Describe:

_____
_____
_____
_____
_____
_____

☐ Other

Describe:

_____
_____
_____
_____
_____
_____

Objectives for CVE programs targeting community members or communities that influence those at risk for extremism

☐ Help community members understand and identify violent extremism and risks (e.g., raise awareness of extremism).

Describe:

_____
_____
_____
_____
_____
_____

Chapter Two: Core Components and Logic Model

**Worksheet 2.1
Identifying Core Components**

☐ Build the capacity of community members to identify/engage with at-risk individuals (e.g., engagements that seek to help the community understand, confront, and respond to violent extremism).

Describe:

_____
_____
_____
_____
_____

☐ Build the capacity of positive and influential community members and leaders to credibly counter violent extremist ideology (e.g., leadership training, social media training, building capacity of nongovernmental organizations or private volunteer organizations).

Describe:

_____
_____
_____
_____
_____

☐ Create environments that are accepting of minority groups (e.g., enhance understanding of, collaboration with, and tolerance of minority groups).

Describe:

_____
_____
_____
_____
_____

RAND Program Evaluation Toolkit for Countering Violent Extremism

Worksheet 2.1
Identifying Core Components

☐ Promote policies that address political grievances (e.g., enhance legal protections, protect against discrimination and hate crimes against populations with minority members who may be at risk for extremism).

Describe:

_____
_____
_____
_____
_____

☐ Strengthen government capacity to curtail violent extremism (e.g., build the capacity of law enforcement to identify, investigate, and prosecute terrorism cases; enhance government/law enforcement cultural understanding of at-risk groups; enhance community policing; improve U.S. domestic counterterrorism policies; raise government/law enforcement awareness and understanding of extremism).

Describe:

_____
_____
_____
_____
_____

☐ Other

Describe:

_____
_____
_____
_____
_____

Chapter Two: Core Components and Logic Model

Worksheet 2.1
Identifying Core Components

Next, we'll need to combine the descriptions of *activities* and *objectives* into well-specified bullets that describe the two together. Below are examples of well-specified and poorly specified program activities and objectives.

Poorly Specified Example	Well-Specified Example
• Messages that counter extremist narratives	• Use Twitter and other social media platforms to spread a message advocating interracial acceptance.
• Train religious leaders	• Train local religious leaders in Dallas, Texas, to identify signs of radicalization and directly engage with at-risk youth.

Describe activities and objectives in single, well-specified bullet points:

_____
_____
_____
_____
_____
_____
_____
_____
_____
_____

Program Outputs

Program outputs are the amount, quality, or volume of goods or services provided by the program. These outputs can help measure a program's performance. Some common measures of outputs for each type of activity are shown in **Figure 2.2**.

RAND Program Evaluation Toolkit for Countering Violent Extremism

Worksheet 2.1
Identifying Core Components

Figure 2.2
Examples of CVE Program Outputs

Activity	Example Output
Communication	Quantity of materials produced or distributed (e.g., number of tweets)
Training/education	Number of trainings delivered or number of personnel trained
Counseling	Number of people counseled, number of counseling sessions per participant
Group activities	Number of participants enrolled, number of events held, average participation per event

5. What are the outputs provided by the program? Specify:

☐ Were any materials developed as part of the program?

Describe:

_____
_____
_____
_____
_____
_____

☐ Were any individuals trained as part of the program?

Describe:

_____
_____
_____
_____
_____
_____

Chapter Two: Core Components and Logic Model

**Worksheet 2.1
Identifying Core Components**

☐ Were any individuals provided with services as part of the program?

Describe:

_____
_____
_____
_____
_____
_____
_____

☐ Were there any other program outputs?

Describe:

_____
_____
_____
_____
_____
_____
_____

Next, we'll need to transform these descriptions into well-specified bullets that describe program outputs. Below is an example of a well-specified and a poorly specified program output.

Poorly Specified Example	Well-Specified Example
• Program trained youth.	• Program conducted five social media trainings in Detroit, training 20 15- to 18-year-olds in three months to help them more effectively counter violent extremism.

25

RAND Program Evaluation Toolkit for Countering Violent Extremism

Worksheet 2.1
Identifying Core Components

Describe activities and outputs using single, well-specified bullet points:

_____
_____
_____
_____
_____
_____
_____
_____
_____
_____
_____

Intended Outcomes

Outcomes are changes in the target population expected as a result of engaging in the program activities. These outcomes may include changes in knowledge, attitudes, skills, or behaviors and should be directly related to the needs being filled. Effective outcomes follow the SMART criteria (Lesesne et al., 2011). That is, they should be

- **S**pecific: Describe precisely what is expected to change and for whom.
- **M**easurable: There must be a way to determine the presence or extent of change.
- **A**chievable: Outcomes must be feasible for the target population (e.g., based on prior empirical expectations for change).
- **R**ealistic: Outcomes should be able to be accomplished with the available resources.
- **T**ime-bound: The change is expected to occur within a specific time frame.

Chapter Two: Core Components and Logic Model

Worksheet 2.1
Identifying Core Components

5. What are the intended outcomes of the program? Specify:

☐ What is expected to change (e.g., perceptions of political violence, levels of anger, perceptions of the availability of social support, attitudes toward police, sense of community, perceived quality of life)?

Describe:

_____
_____
_____
_____
_____
_____
_____
_____

☐ What target population is expected to change? (Use the well-specified bullet from the "Target Population" section of this worksheet.)

Describe:

_____
_____
_____
_____
_____
_____
_____
_____

RAND Program Evaluation Toolkit for Countering Violent Extremism

Worksheet 2.1
Identifying Core Components

☐ In what time frame do you expect the change to occur (e.g., perceptions of the availability of social support may change after a workshop or video screening)?

Describe:

_____
_____
_____
_____
_____
_____
_____
_____
_____

☐ How much do you expect the intended outcome to change?

Describe:

_____
_____
_____
_____
_____
_____
_____
_____
_____

Outcomes can be grouped into short-term and long-term outcomes. According to a leading source on evaluations, "Short-term outcomes should be attainable within 1 to 3 years, while longer-term outcomes should be achievable within a 4 to 6 year timeframe" (W. K. Kellogg Foundation, 2000). However, these standards are not set in stone: If your program is only three months long, your short-term outcomes may occur in a one- to three-month time frame, and your long-term outcomes may occur in a six-month to one-year time frame. Anchor your short- and long-term outcomes to your program's length: What do you expect to change immedi-

Chapter Two: Core Components and Logic Model

Worksheet 2.1
Identifying Core Components

ately, and what do you expect that this immediate change will bring about? For example, a workshop may train community members on warning signs of extremism; immediately, you might expect knowledge to increase, but in the long term you expect behaviors to change—for example, more people are able to someone exhibiting signs of extremism and then act on it. Think about your short- and long-term outcomes. Then, transform these descriptions into well-specified bullets that describe intended program outcomes and group them as short-term and long-term outcomes. Below is an example of a well-specified and a poorly specified program outcome.

Poorly Specified Example	Well-Specified Example
• Increase knowledge about violent extremism.	• After Springfield High School students participate in the training workshop, at least 80% of students will be able to score 75% or higher on a test about elements associated with violent extremism.

Describe the intended short-term outcomes using well-specified bullets:

_____
_____
_____
_____
_____
_____
_____
_____
_____
_____
_____

RAND Program Evaluation Toolkit for Countering Violent Extremism

Worksheet 2.1
Identifying Core Components

Describe the intended long-term outcomes using well-specified bullets:

_____
_____
_____
_____
_____
_____
_____
_____
_____
_____

Current Evaluation Activities

You may have already thought about evaluating your program or begun collecting data to inform an evaluation of your program. These activities may help inform your evaluation design. If you are not currently conducting any evaluation activities, leave this section blank and skip to next section ("Needs Being Addressed by the Program").

6. Summarize any activities you are conducting to inform an evaluation of your program:

_____
_____
_____
_____
_____
_____
_____
_____

Chapter Two: Core Components and Logic Model

Worksheet 2.1
Identifying Core Components

Next, we'll need to transform these descriptions into well-specified bullets that describe your program's current evaluation activities. Below are examples of well-specified and poorly specified evaluation activities.

Poorly Specified Example	Well-Specified Example
• Tracking changes in attitudes toward violent extremist groups	• Assess changes in the degree to which program participants sympathize with violent extremist groups. • Track each participant's attendance at the eight program sessions.

Describe the evaluation activities using well-specified bullet points:

_____
_____
_____
_____
_____
_____
_____
_____
_____
_____

Needs Being Addressed by the Program

Needs represent a problem or deficiency in the community that the program intends to remedy. Needs are closely aligned with, but distinct from, the objectives you specified in the activities and objectives sections above. For example, a program objective may be to "enhance positive social networks" for individuals at risk of violent extremism; the need that is addressed may be that either (1) individuals *without* strong networks are particularly vulnerable to violent extremist recruiting, or (2) positive networks buffer against extremist messages and activities that may entice groups of individuals to adopt extremist ideologies or join larger extremist

31

RAND Program Evaluation Toolkit for Countering Violent Extremism

Worksheet 2.1
Identifying Core Components

groups. The long-term goal of the program is to fill one or more of these needs. Because we have very little information on the causes of violent extremism, the needs that CVE programs are intended to address are often intentionally broad, but they are more specific than the ultimate goal of preventing violent extremism.

Ideally, there are some data pointing to a particular need for your program. For example, a program to reduce high school dropouts has some evidence that a significant proportion of youth in a community do not finish school. Such data in the field of violent extremism are scarce. Nonetheless, thinking through the needs that your program addresses is a useful exercise to help evaluate your program. Some examples of the needs met by CVE programs may include the following:

- Increased proliferation of extremist messaging and recruiting
- Lack of knowledge/awareness about the signs and symptoms of extremism
- Lack of competence in helping individuals who are vulnerable to extremist messaging and recruiting; competence refers to an understanding of how to approach and talk with someone who might be engaging with extremist networks and organizations
- Significant numbers of community members who are vulnerable to extremist networks and recruiting
- Community conditions that increase vulnerability to extremist networks and recruiting
- Negative attitudes toward conventional community resources (e.g., clergy, law enforcement)
- Lack of adequate care/support for at-risk individuals
- Barriers to accessing available resources.

Once you've thought about the specific needs your program addresses, create well-specified bullets that describe those needs. Below are examples of well-specified and poorly specified needs.

Poorly Specified Example	Well-Specified Example
• Vulnerable community members	• High school completion rates in St. Louis are declining, which may increase the number of individuals who are vulnerable to extremist messaging.
• Lack of knowledge about signs and symptoms of extremism	• A focus group with law enforcement officials revealed a lack of awareness about right-wing extremist groups known to be present in the region.

32

Chapter Two: Core Components and Logic Model

Worksheet 2.1
Identifying Core Components

Describe the needs addressed by the program using well-specified bullet points:

RAND Program Evaluation Toolkit for Countering Violent Extremism

Use Core Components to Build a Logic Model

Logic models facilitate the visualization of relationships between the core components of a program. Read from left to right, these models depict the logical flow from inputs (resources) to actions (activities) to outputs (outcomes) to assessment (evaluation) to goals (needs). An "if . . . then" relationship connects adjacent components: If the resources are provided, then the activities are conducted; if the activities are conducted, then the targeted population can participate; if the targeted population participates, then the outcomes can occur.

Reason for Building a Logic Model

A logic model benefits a program in three primary ways:

- It simplifies and summarizes the program's core components.
- It depicts the connection between concrete resources/activities and abstract goals.
- It allows programs to assess how well a plan aligns with actual implementation.

Now that you have identified and specified the core components of your program, you can use the responses from **Worksheet 2.1** to construct a program logic model using **Template 2.1**. The bullets in each summary section of **Worksheet 2.1** can be transferred directly to the corresponding section of the logic model in **Template 2.1**. A sample completed logic model for a fictional program is shown in **Template 2.2**.

34

Chapter Two: Core Components and Logic Model

Template 2.1
Blank Program Logic Model Template

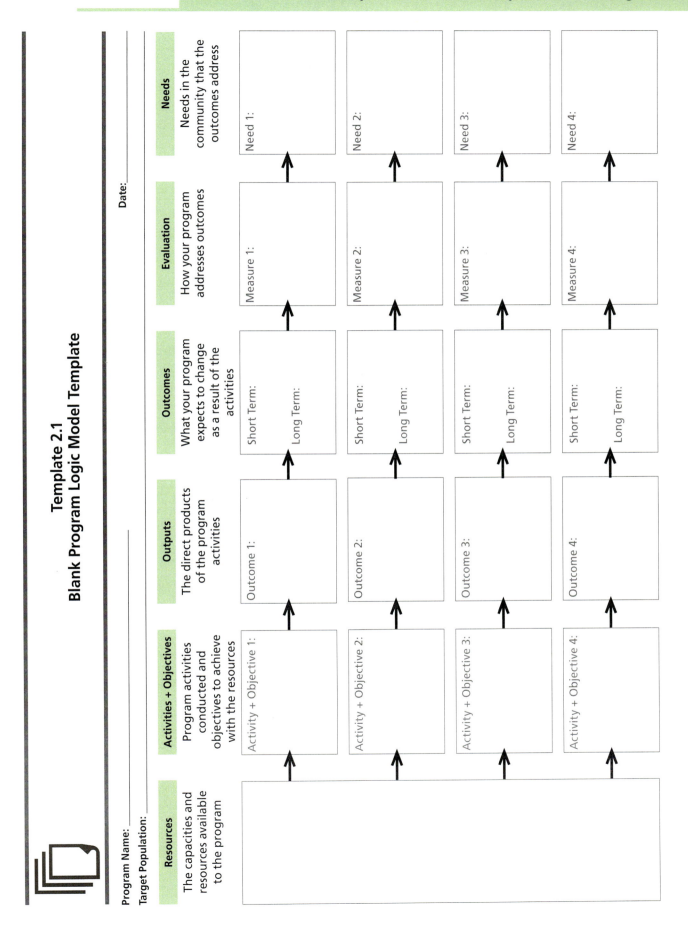

RAND Program Evaluation Toolkit for Countering Violent Extremism

Template 2.2
Sample Program Logic Model

Program Name: Countering Violent Extremism Internet training
Target Population: Parents
Date: _____

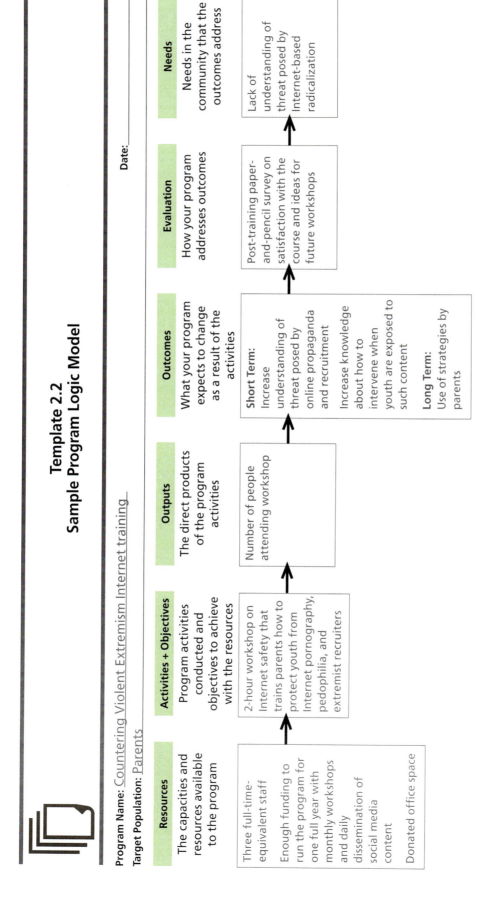

Chapter Two: Core Components and Logic Model

Assess the Quality of Your Program's Logic Model

Reasons to Assess Quality

An effective logic model provides an accurate and comprehensive representation of a program. To be effective, a logic model must be complete and detailed. Because the logic model serves as the foundation for your program's evaluation, it is essential that you take the time to develop a complete a detailed logic model. If a program cannot articulate its core components in a logic model, that may be an indicator that the program's activities are not well specified or concrete enough to merit an evaluation at this time.

In addition, the relationships between the program's core components must be reasonably clear: If the target population participates, then the outputs will be completed; if the outputs are completed, then the outcomes could be possible; if the outcomes are possible, then they can be evaluated through assessment; if the evaluation is completed, then we will know whether the needs of the community were successfully addressed. To ensure that your program's evaluation is reasonable and appropriate, you must ensure that the core components of your logic model align with one another.

How to Assess Quality

Use the following checklists to review the logic model you created using **Template 2.1**. Check off each item that is true for your logic model (W. K. Kellogg Foundation, 2000).

37

RAND Program Evaluation Toolkit for Countering Violent Extremism

Checklist 2.1
Is Your Logic Model Complete and Appropriately Detailed?

☐ All significant *resources* contributing to the program are listed.[1]

☐ All significant *activities* contributing to the program are listed.[2]

☐ All people intended to use the program are represented in the listed *target population(s)*.

☐ The listed *target population* specifies the relevant age group, gender, and other characteristics.

☐ The listed *target population* provides enough detail that it is clear which subgroups are intentionally excluded from participation in the program.

☐ *Outcomes* are SMART (specific, measurable, achievable, reasonable, and time-bound).

☐ All significant *evaluation activities* used to assess the program are listed.

☐ Any significant community *needs* addressed by the program are listed.

If you did not check off all of these items, revisit the corresponding section in **Template 2.1** to further specify your program's core components. For example, if you did not check the first item, "All significant resources contributing to the program are listed," revisit the "Resources" section of **Worksheet 2.1**.

---

[1] Significant resources are the resources (e.g., money, staff, equipment, supplies) that are essential to and contribute the majority of support to the program activities. Use your best judgment to identify these resources.

[2] Significant activities are the defining activities that make up the essence or core of your program.

Chapter Two: Core Components and Logic Model

**Checklist 2.2
Are the Core Components of Your
Logic Model Appropriately Aligned?**

1. *Resources* **are adequate and suitable to conduct program** *activities.*

☐ Yes ⟶ This means that you have appropriate and adequate staff, space, and materials to fully implement your program.

☐ No ⟶ Without adequate resources, your program may not have the desired outcomes. Before implementing your program, you need to secure all necessary resources. For example, if you need a religious leader for your program but do not have access to one, this means that you do not have adequate resources.

2. The program *activities* **involve the** *targeted population.*

☐ Yes ⟶ This means that your program activities are reaching the target population.

☐ No ⟶ If your program activities do not reach your target population, your program will not have the desired outcomes. You may need to reconsider whether you have identified the appropriate target population or augment your program with additional activities that reach the intended population. For example, if your program is targeting former prisoners reentering the community, you will need a way to identify and recruit those individuals to your program.

3. *Outputs* **correspond to the** *program activities* **listed.**

☐ Yes ⟶ This means that you have captured the level of effort for each of your program activities. Each of your activities should have an output. All outputs should be tied to at least one or more program activities.

☐ No ⟶ If you have an output listed that is not linked to a program activity, you may be missing a program activity. If you have a program activity without an output, add an output for that activity. All program activities should have at least one output, and, similarly, all outputs should be tied to one or more program activities.

RAND Program Evaluation Toolkit for Countering Violent Extremism

Checklist 2.2
Are the Core Components of Your Logic Model Appropriately Aligned?

4. *Outcomes* correspond to *program activities* listed.

☐ Yes ⟶ This means that you have identified which of the activities contribute to each of your program outcomes. You do not want to overreach in identifying outcomes that are grander or more comprehensive than the program activities. Ensuring that your activities and outcomes are closely aligned is what allows your program evaluation to accurately assess the impact of the program's activities.

☐ No ⟶ If the outcomes are not directly tied to program activities, you may need to reconsider whether you have identified the appropriate outcomes. For example, if you are implementing a training on refuting extremist messages, it is unlikely to improve law enforcement officers' ability to build constructive relationships with community members. Before beginning a program evaluation, be sure the program activities and outcomes are closely aligned.

5. *Outcomes* fall reasonably within the *time frame* of the program.

☐ Yes ⟶ This means that the length of the program is sufficient to result in the changes listed in your logic model. You do not want to overreach in identifying outcomes that fall far outside the program's time frame because they are hard to detect. For example, if your program is targeting adolescents, you do not want to list outcomes that will not occur until these adolescents become adults.

☐ No ⟶ If the outcomes fall outside the time frame of the program, you may need to reconsider whether you have identified the appropriate outcomes. Identifying outcomes that are occur close to the conclusion of the program makes the connection between program activities and outcomes stronger. Long-term follow-up may be an option for your program, but you should consider short-term outcomes first.

6. *Evaluation methods* are reasonable, given the *resources* and *time frame*.

☐ Yes ⟶ This means that you have the resources (e.g., time, money, staff) and expertise to both collect and analyze your evaluation data and that you have linked the timing of the evaluation with the timing of the program. For example, if your program is a two-month training, the evaluation data collection would need to begin before the program and end no sooner than the end of the program.

Chapter Two: Core Components and Logic Model

**Checklist 2.2
Are the Core Components of Your
Logic Model Appropriately Aligned?**

☐ No ⟶ If your evaluation methods are not reasonable, given your resources and expertise, consider hiring an external evaluator. For example, university faculty and graduate students can provide support for evaluation design and data analysis. If you do not have the resources to hire an external evaluator, consider whether you can simplify your evaluation design to fit with your program's resources and staff expertise. Before implementing an evaluation, be sure you have the resources and expertise to do so.

7. Evaluation measures provide appropriate assessments of the program *outcomes*.

☐ Yes ⟶ This means that each program outcome has one or more evaluation measures associated with it.

☐ No ⟶ **Chapter Four** can help you identify evaluation measures to capture your program outcomes. If you do not have the resources to collect measures for all program outcomes, you can choose those that are most important to the program and its funders or those that are most indicative of program success. However, this limits your ability to capture the full impact of your CVE program.

8. *Outcomes* correspond to the community *needs* listed.

☐ Yes ⟶ This means that your program outcomes are helping to address an identified need. For example, if your program trains parents of junior and senior high school students to identify youth who are at high risk for violent extremism, it should help address a shortage of training in that area. Your program should not be competing with many other programs doing the same thing.

☐ No ⟶ If your program outcomes do not fill a need, your program may have trouble recruiting participants because it is competing with similar programs. Consider whether your investment of resources in the program could be redirected to focus on an area where there is an identified need.

If you did not check "Yes" to all of these items, you may need to calibrate the core components of your program. Revising your outcomes to more realistically reflect your program activities is a common way to improve alignment. For example, a training program that does not measure knowledge and changes in targeted behaviors would have a poor evaluation design.

RAND Program Evaluation Toolkit for Countering Violent Extremism

Summary

Congratulations, you have completed the first interactive chapter of the toolkit! This chapter provided guidance on how to develop a logic model (**Worksheet 2.1**) that will be used in subsequent chapters to plan the program evaluation. The core program component you identified in your logic model will be used to help you select evaluation measures and ensure that the time frame of your evaluation reflects program activities. Now that you have a complete logic model (**Template 2.1**) and have reviewed it using **Checklists 2.1** and **2.2**, you are ready to begin designing your CVE program evaluation. Chapter Three will provide you with guidance about the type of evaluation design that is appropriate for your CVE program and walk you through a series of interactive worksheets to ensure that you consider the factors that may influence your CVE program's evaluation design, such as resources, timing of evaluation data collection, and data sensitivity.

Chapter Three: Evaluation Design

Chapter Three
Design an Evaluation for Your Program

In this chapter, we discuss several key issues to consider when selecting an evaluation design and drafting an evaluation plan. The chapter concludes with a review of the quality of information in the draft evaluation plan.

Objective:

To provide guidance about the type of evaluation that is appropriate for your program.

Learn the Types of Evaluation Designs

To help you select an evaluation design, we first provide some information on different types of evaluation designs and the expertise, cost, and ease of each. Below are the five most common types of evaluation designs, listed from least to most rigorous:

1. *Retrospective pre-/post-intervention evaluation.* This type of evaluation involves collecting data from program participants at only one time point but asking them how their skills, knowledge, or behavior has changed since before the program.
2. *Pre-/post-intervention evaluation.* This type of evaluation involves collecting data from program participants at two time points: before the program starts and after the program ends.
3. *Interrupted time-series analysis.* This approach uses secondary data (e.g., census data, school data) to assess changes at multiple time points before and after the program.
4. *Pre-/post-intervention evaluation with comparison group.* This is the same as a pre-/post-intervention evaluation (number 2), except that you also collect data from a group that did not participate in the program but is similar in composition to the participating group.

RAND Program Evaluation Toolkit for Countering Violent Extremism

5. *Pre-/post-intervention evaluation with control group.* This type of evaluation requires you to randomly assign your pool of program participants to either participate in the program (intervention group) or not participate in the program (control group), then collect data at two time points: before the program starts and after the program ends.

When deciding on a type of evaluation design, you must consider the ease of execution, confidence in the evaluation result, cost of the design, and the expertise needed to gather and use the evaluation data. As mentioned earlier, these designs are presented from the least rigorous (retrospective pre-/post-intervention evaluation) to the most rigorous (pre-/post-intervention evaluation with control group). Select the most rigorous design that your program has the money and expertise to implement. Ease of execution describes the relative ease of each evaluation design. However, remember that even a retrospective pre/post design can provide you with valuable data on the effectiveness of your program and ways that it can be improved. **Table 3.1** summarizes the characteristics of each design.

Identify Issues Pertinent to Your Evaluation Design

Several factors influence program evaluation design: (1) the number of program participants, (2) selecting a control or comparison group, (3) the timing of the evaluation and the intended audience, (4) data security and human subjects protection, (5) evaluation expertise, and (6) resources available for the evaluation. In the following sections, we introduce a number of issues to consider for each of these factors. **Worksheet 3.1** provides a place for you to record notes about your CVE program that may be relevant to each of these factors.

Number of Program Participants

The number of program participants depends on the outcomes you are measuring. If you are looking for a statistically significant effect (an effect that you are confident did not occur by chance), the number of participants in the evaluation or your sample size would be related to your ability to statistically detect an effect. You will need to take into account several things when conducting your evaluation:

- What do you expect to change as a result of the program?
- How many people could you enroll in your evaluation?
- Are there previous evaluation studies of similar programs that can be used to estimate program effects?
- How are the intended outcomes of your program related to one another?

These factors will influence your ability to document a statistically significant effect, and consulting a statistician would help you to determine an adequate number of participants for your evaluation. There are statistical models that can help identify an adequate number based on the program's expected effects.

It is important to note that program evaluations are often not about detecting statistical significance. For example, program staff may set benchmarks (e.g., 20 percent of participants) or be more focused on determining whether clients move into a different clinical range between the program's beginning and end.

Chapter Three: Evaluation Design

Table 3.1
Types of Evaluation Designs

Method	Ease of Execution	Confidence in Result	Cost	Expertise Needed to Gather and Use Data
Retrospective pre-/post-intervention evaluation	Easier than the standard pre/post evaluation	Only moderate confidence that the program caused the change, *and* it may be hard for participants to recall how they were at the start	Inexpensive	Low
Pre-/post-intervention evaluation	Easy way to measure change	Only moderate confidence that the program caused the change	Moderate	Moderate
Interrupted time series analysis	Requires several years of data collected in the same way, which can be hard to find	Tracks short- and long-term changes, but one cannot be sure that the program caused the change	Inexpensive (data usually collected by other sources)	Low (for simple graphical technique; statistical methods are complex)
Pre-/post-intervention evaluation with comparison group	Can be hard to find group that is similar to program group	Provides good level of confidence that the program caused the change	High; doubles the cost of the evaluation	Moderate to high
Pre-/post-intervention evaluation with control group	Hard to find group willing to be randomly assigned; ethical issues of withholding beneficial program from control participants	Provides excellent level of confidence that the program caused the change	High; doubles the cost of the evaluation	High

45

RAND Program Evaluation Toolkit for Countering Violent Extremism

Selecting a Control or Comparison Group

In pre-/post-intervention evaluations with either control or comparison groups, most evidence is derived from comparing the group participating in the program with nonparticipants. Selecting nonparticipants can be difficult. In the most rigorous designs, all participants eligible for the program are randomly assigned to either participate or not; those not assigned to the program are the control group. Randomizing participants to these groups helps ensure that the two groups are as similar to each other as possible. Often, programs put individuals in the control group on a waiting list and offer the same services to these individuals after the evaluation is over. Randomizing people to the groups being compared can be challenging, however, so we suggest consulting with an evaluation expert.

If randomization is not feasible or desirable, one can still learn a great deal from a comparison population that did not participate in the program. The goal here is to replicate randomization as much as possible. This means that you should select a group that looks as similar as possible to the group that receives the intervention. For example, if you are offering training to high school teachers, you might offer the program in one high school and select as a comparison group another high school in the same or a similar community. Again, this does not mean that the comparison group never receives the intervention and, in fact, you can offer the program to the comparison group after the evaluation has ended.

Timing of Evaluation and Intended Audience

The length of the program and the anticipated timeline for the evaluation both have implications for the timing of the evaluation. It is better to begin an evaluation before beginning to implement the program so you can collect some data from participants before they are involved with the program. You also want to collect data after their participation in the program ends (e.g., after they have received training or seen marketing campaign materials). However, the timing of that data collection depends on the length of the program. For example, coordinators of an eight-week training program for religious leaders might want to collect evaluation data right before the training begins (week 1) and right after the training ends (week 8). Coordinators of a media campaign will also want to collect data before the campaign commences. However, they may want to hold off on the outcome assessment or collecting more data until the campaign has been operating for several months to allow the campaign to fully reach the target audience.

Important grant and funding deadlines and reporting requirements may also drive the timing of the evaluation. To ensure that your program's evaluation is timed appropriately, you must first identify the intended audience for the evaluation. How will the evaluation findings be used? For example, findings could be included in applications for new grant funding, progress reporting on existing grants, annual organizational reports, or briefings to a board of directors, community leadership group, program staff, or program participants. If your program plans to use the evaluation findings in a variety of ways, identify the earliest point that the evaluation would need to be completed and use that as an anchor for timing your evaluation.

When making decisions about the program evaluation design, consider the following questions, drawn from **Worksheet 3.1**:

- When does the evaluation need to be completed? This question will help you identify a deadline for completing your evaluation.
- Does the program have an end date? This question will help you identify the timing for post-intervention data collection.
- Is the program cyclical (e.g., run for eight weeks twice a year)? This question will also help you identify the timing for data collection to coincide with program cycles.
  - If yes, when is the next time the program will be offered?
  - If no, how many months has the program been operating?
- How will the evaluation data be used? This question will help you identify ways to report your evaluation findings (e.g., a presentation or briefing to the board, a report to your funder).

Data Security and Human Subjects Protection

Evaluation studies of CVE programs often involve working with human subjects. Protecting program participants from harm during an evaluation (including the disclosure of personal information) is of primary importance for any evaluation that collects data related to program activities or violent extremism. The foundation of human subjects research and its protections in the United States is summarized in the Belmont Report, produced in 1979. This report establishes three basic principles for human subjects research:

1. Respect for persons: Individuals are fully informed that they are participating in research, and voluntary consent is elicited.
2. Beneficence: Research should maximize public benefit and minimize personal harms.
3. Justice: The distribution of research participation opportunities, benefits, and burdens is fair.

The Belmont report applies these principles to research in the form of requirements of informed consent, assessment of risks and benefits, and selection of subjects. Additional requirements are contained in the Common Rule: The U.S. Department of Homeland Security and many other federal agencies apply all elements of the Common Rule to their human subjects research. You may want to review the principles of human subjects research contained in the Belmont Report and the Common Rule (in the Code of Federal Regulations; see the references list at the end of this toolkit for links to both resources).

Evaluation Expertise

Evaluation expertise refers to knowledge and experience in conducting program evaluation. Programs that cannot access evaluation expertise will be limited in the types of evaluation approaches they can feasibly implement. Evaluation expertise can come from academic partners, community-based private and nonprofit organizations, and in-house staff. Often, programs do not have staff or partners with the needed evaluation expertise.

When designing your program's evaluation, consider the type of evaluation expertise available:

- Do any program staff have evaluation expertise?
- Does the program have established relationships with any academic institutions or community-based organizations with evaluation expertise?

If your program does not have program staff with evaluation expertise or established relationships with organizations that can provide evaluation expertise, you might consider engaging an external evaluator to help support your evaluation efforts. The American Evaluation Association provides a searchable database of members available for evaluation consulting (see the references list at the end of this toolkit for a link to its "Find an Evaluator" database).

Available Evaluation Resources

All evaluations require resources. Resources can include supplies and equipment (e.g., access to computers, money for photocopies), staff time, financial resources (e.g., money to support an online survey subscription), and organizational resources (e.g., buy-in from leadership). In addition to the resources your program has set aside for the evaluation, you may be able to leverage additional resources from programs, institutions, and organizations in your community. Understanding the resources available in your community can help save your program time and money and prevent duplication of effort. To help design your evaluation, consider the following:

- What kinds of resources does your program have to support the evaluation?
- What other resources are available in your community that could be used to support the evaluation?

Chapter Three: Evaluation Design

Worksheet 3.1
Issues to Consider for My Program

Reflect on the questions below; they lay out some key issues that you will need to consider when designing your CVE program evaluation.

Detecting a Program Effect

- What is expected to change as a result of the program?
- How many people could you enroll in your evaluation?
- Are there previous evaluation studies of similar programs that can be used to estimate the size of program effects?
- If you have more than one outcome, how are they related to one another?

Your notes:

_____
_____
_____
_____
_____
_____

Timing of Evaluation and Intended Audience

- When does the evaluation need to be completed?
- Does the program have an end date?
- Is the program cyclical (e.g., runs for eight weeks twice a year)?
    - If yes, when is the next time that the program will be offered?
    - If no, how many months has the program been operating?
- How will the evaluation data be used?

Your notes:

_____
_____
_____
_____
_____
_____

RAND Program Evaluation Toolkit for Countering Violent Extremism

Worksheet 3.1
Issues to Consider for My Program

Data Security and Human-Subjects Protection

- Are human participants providing data, and are they doing so willingly and voluntarily?
- Are efforts in place to minimize potential harms to participants (including breaches in privacy) and to maximize public benefits?
- Is the distribution of research opportunities, benefits, and burdens fair?

Your notes:

_____
_____
_____
_____
_____
_____

Evaluation Expertise

- Do any program staff have evaluation expertise?
- Does the program have established relationships with any organizations with evaluation expertise?

Your notes:

_____
_____
_____
_____
_____
_____
_____

Chapter Three: Evaluation Design

Worksheet 3.1
Issues to Consider for My Program

Available Evaluation Resources

- What kinds of resources does your program have to support the evaluation?
- What other resources are available in your community that could be used to support the evaluation?

Your notes:

_____
_____
_____
_____
_____
_____
_____

Select an Evaluation Design

Next, based on your answers to the questions in **Worksheet 3.1**, fill in a portion of your program's evaluation plan (see **Template 3.1**). In the "Sample" column, specify the target population and estimated number of program participants (i.e., sample size) for the evaluation. In the "Data Collection" column, first specify the timing of your evaluation (i.e., the date or dates that data collection will occur). Again, these should be tied to the beginning and end dates of your evaluation. In the "Plan for Data Analysis" column, specify the intended audience for the evaluation and any specific plans you have for sharing the findings with this audience (e.g., "Present a briefing at the May 11 board meeting").

At this point, the field for frequency in the "Data Collection" column and the "Measures" column should remain blank. You will continue to add details to your evaluation plan in subsequent chapters. Information about available resources and evaluation expertise will be used to select evaluation measures and an analysis strategy.

RAND Program Evaluation Toolkit for Countering Violent Extremism

Template 3.1
Evaluation Planner

Sample	Data Collection	Measures	Plan for Data Analysis	Resources Needed
Target population	Timing		Intended audience	
Size	Frequency			
	Person responsible			

Chapter Three: Evaluation Design

Assess the Quality of the Design

Use the following checklist (W. K. Kellogg Foundation, 2000) to review the information in **Worksheet 3.1**, your draft evaluation plan. Check off each item that is true for your draft evaluation. To help connect the **Checklist 3.1** with **Template 3.1**, we have italicized the terms that appear in both.

Checklist 3.1
Does Your Evaluation Plan Consider the Following Factors?

☐ Whether your *sample size* will allow you to detect a statistically or otherwise meaningful impact of your program (note that you may need the help of a statistician or evaluation expert to help determine whether your sample size is adequate)

☐ How the length of the program may influence your *data collection timing*

☐ Whether the evaluation will answer questions of interest to the *intended audience(s)* for the evaluation

☐ How grant and funding deadlines and reporting requirements may influence the *timing of the data collection*

☐ How the evaluation data will be used

☐ Respect, beneficence, and protection of evaluation participants.

Summary

This chapter provided guidance about planning an evaluation that will be appropriate for your program based on its activities and available resources and expertise (**Worksheet 3.1**). Now that you have completed this chapter, you should have a partially complete evaluation plan (**Template 3.1**) that carefully considers a variety of key issues (**Checklist 3.1**). You can complete the evaluation plan by stepping through the remainder of the toolkit chapters. **Chapter Four** will help you select process and outcome evaluation measures.

Chapter Four: Evaluation Measures

Chapter Four
Select Evaluation Measures for Your Program

Objective:
To support the selection of measures that are appropriate for your program evaluation.

This chapter first defines process and outcome evaluation measures and explains why it is important to collect *both* types of evaluation measures. Then, it presents process and outcome measures used in prior evaluations of CVE programs or related interventions as possible options for use in your program's evaluation. The chapter concludes with a review of the measures selected to ensure that they are appropriate for your program and the available level of resources and evaluation expertise.

Select Process Evaluation Measures

Process evaluation is a form of program evaluation designed to document and analyze the early development and actual implementation of a program, assessing whether and how well services are delivered as intended or planned. Process evaluation is also known as implementation assessment (Wholey, Hatry, and Newcomer, 2010; Rossi, Lipsey, and Freeman, 2004). Process data can include

- Tracking participation or attendance
- Tracking participants (collecting demographic data on participants)
- Participant satisfaction surveys
- Measures of implementation activities (program fidelity measures, such as adherence to the program curriculum).

RAND Program Evaluation Toolkit for Countering Violent Extremism

Reasons for Process Evaluation

Measuring the quality of program implementation can answer questions such as the following:

- How much of the program were participants exposed to?
- What are the characteristics of program participants?
- How satisfied are participants and program staff?
- Was the program implemented as intended?

A process evaluation may enhance your understanding of why program outcomes were or were not achieved. For example, if a training program intended to significantly increase parents' comfort in talking to their children about violent extremism, but the outcome evaluation indicated that this program did not have the intended outcomes (e.g., no parents reported having discussions with their children), program staff may conclude that the training program was ineffective.

Process evaluation data could help enrich the interpretation of these findings. If *attendance data* revealed that only 30 percent of program participants attended four or more of eight sessions, program staff may want to reanalyze the data to look only at individuals who attended all or almost all of the program sessions. Improving program retention may be a necessary first step before program effects can be detected.

Demographic data can also be useful in providing insight into whether the population served by the program reflects the intended target population. For example, if demographic data reveal that 25 percent of program participants were outside the program's expected audience, program staff may want to reanalyze the data to look only at participants within the expected age range. For example, you may find that the parents who participated tended to have younger children, so the types of outcomes you were looking for did not have time to actualize. You may also find that the program works well for fathers but not mothers or vice versa. To look for these types of subgroup differences, you will need to collect demographic data.

Participant or program staff dissatisfaction can minimize program outcomes (e.g., by limiting the amount of knowledge that participants gain during the program). If program participants report being extremely dissatisfied with their experience with the program, program staff may wish to reanalyze the data to determine the extent to which dissatisfaction increased as program outcomes decreased or to identify sources of dissatisfaction that could be addressed. Additionally, it may be difficult to sustain a program when participants are dissatisfied.

Finally, assessing *program fidelity* can show whether the implementation adheres to the program's original design (Smith, Daunic, and Taylor, 2007). If fidelity data reveal that program staff were not fully implementing the required curriculum, improving the fidelity of implementation may be a necessary first step before program effects can be detected. For example, evaluations often find that program effects diminish over time, and one reason for this is often that the program was implemented with less fidelity to the original design.

Possible Options Used in Prior Evaluation Studies

Understanding process evaluation measures that were used by other programs could help you identify evaluation measures that will be useful for your program. Based on our literature review, we identified sample process measures that could be used in evaluations of CVE pro-

Chapter Four: Evaluation Measures

grams (see **Table 4.1**). These measures are organized according to the four program activities described in Chapter Two to make it easier for you to identify measures that are relevant for the type of CVE program you are implementing. After you review the sample measures, specify which of the process evaluation measures your program plans to use in **Template 3.1**, your evaluation plan.

Table 4.1
Sample Process Measures

Sample Measure	Brief Description	Reference
Communication	Number of campaigns completed	U.S. Agency for International Development (USAID), 2011
	Number of media hits	Poister, 2010
	Percentage target population that is aware of campaign	Rossi, Lipsey, and Freeman, 2004
	Amount spent on developing and disseminating the campaign	Kettner, Moroney, and Martin, 2013
Training/education	Participant satisfaction with information provided and program personnel	Rossi, Lipsey, and Freeman, 2004
Counseling	Number of trained staff providing services	Kettner, Moroney, and Martin, 2013
	Number of people receiving services	Rossi, Lipsey, and Freeman, 2004
	Number of people receiving services who are intended targets of the services	Rossi, Lipsey, and Freeman, 2004
	Percentage of target population aware of the services	Rossi, Lipsey, and Freeman, 2004
	Participant satisfaction with services and program personnel	Rossi, Lipsey, and Freeman, 2004
Group activities	Number of individuals enrolled	USAID, 2013
	Percent attendance per activity	Sweikhart, Sinclair, and Shafeek, 2010

NOTE: The "Reference" column includes references to source articles describing how the measure was developed or evaluation studies in which the measure was used.

RAND Program Evaluation Toolkit for Countering Violent Extremism

Select Outcome Evaluation Measures

Outcome evaluation is an assessment of how well a program's activities or services have enacted expected changes in the target population or social condition (Rossi, Lipsey, and Freeman, 2004).

Reasons for Outcome Evaluation

Outcome evaluations help program staff determine whether their program is having the desired effect. Measuring program outcomes can answer questions about how participants' knowledge, skills, attitudes, or behaviors have changed as a result of their participation in a CVE program.

Possible Options Used in Prior Evaluation Studies

We identified sample outcome measures used in evaluations of CVE programs. These measures are organized according to the different program objectives identified in Chapter Two to make it easier for you to identify measures that are relevant for the type of CVE program you are implementing. Table 4.2 provides example measures that may be appropriate for interventions focused on individuals at risk of violent extremism. Table 4.3 provides example measures for interventions targeting the community, family, or friends of individuals at risk for violent extremism.

Note that the available measures may not be suitable for your specific program. You may also need to supplement your selected measures with additional and tailored assessments. Consequently, we urge you to also carefully review Appendixes A and B. **Appendix A** provides a brief primer on ways you can create your own survey with specially tailored questions to assess program processes or impact. It also includes a worksheet that provides step-by-step guidance on crafting a survey. **Appendix B** reviews common measures for assessing the reach and impact of social media campaigns.

After you review the sample outcome measures below, as well as Appendixes A and B, specify which of the outcome evaluation measures your program plans to use in **Template 3.1**, your evaluation plan. In the "Measures" column of **Template 3.1**, write a brief description of the measure(s) you have selected. The description can be modeled on those in **Table 4.2**. Also list the reference(s) you will need to acquire for a copy of the measure. Some measures are not included in the articles referenced. To get a copy of these measures, you will need to contact the authors. Contact information for authors can typically be found as a footnote in the articles referenced.

58

Chapter Four: Evaluation Measures

Table 4.2
Sample Outcome Measures for CVE Programs Addressing Individuals at Risk for Violent Extremism

Construct	Measure Name	Example Item	Reference
Objective: Countering violent extremist opinions and ideology			
Outgroup hostility	Normative beliefs about aggression	Making threats against [Jewish] people is . . . 1 = absolutely the right thing to do, 2 = somewhat right, 3 = I am not sure, 4 = somewhat wrong, 5 = completely wrong	Amjad and Wood, 2009
Support for extremism	Support for extremism	True or False? Suicide bombing/other violence against civilians is justified to defend religion from its enemies.	Pew Research Center, 2011
Support for political violence	Support for political violence	True or False? Sending threatening letters to public figures is sometimes necessary to stop dangerous policies.	Zaidise, Canetti-Nisim, and Pedahzur, 2007
Subtle racism	Symbolic Racism 2000 Scale	Strongly agree, agree, disagree, strongly disagree? Discrimination against blacks is no longer a problem in the United States.	Henry and Sears, 2002
Objective: Improve psychological issues, address moral concerns			
Anxiety	Beck Anxiety Inventory	Indicate how much you have been bothered by the symptom during the past month . . . Nervousness 0 = not at all; 1 = mildly, but it doesn't bother me much; 2 = moderately, it wasn't pleasant at time; 3 = severely, it bothered me a lot	Beck et al., 1988
Anger	Clinical Anger Scale	A. I do not feel angry; B. I feel angry; C. I am angry most of the time now; D. I am so angry and hostile all the time that I can't stand it	Snell et al., 1995

**Table 4.2
Sample Outcome Measures for CVE Programs
Addressing Individuals at Risk for Violent Extremism**

Construct	Measure Name	Example Item	Reference
Depression	Center for Epidemiologic Studies Depression Scale–Revised	I felt sad 0 = not at all or less than 1 day; 1 = 1–2 days; 2 = 3–4 days; 3 = 5–7 days; 4 = nearly every day for 2 weeks	Van Dam and Earleywine, 2011
Objective: Enhance positive social networks			
Guidance (receiving advice), reliable alliance (feeling assured that one can rely on others), reassurance of worth (feeling valued by others), opportunity for nurturance (feeling needed to provide nurturance), attachments (receiving a sense of emotional security), and social integration (feeling a sense of belonging in a group)	Social Provisions Scale	There are people I can depend on to help me if I really need it. 1 = strongly disagree, 2 = disagree, 3 = agree, 4 = strongly agree	Cutrona and Russell, 1987
Confidant support and affective support	The Duke–University of North Carolina Functional Social Support Questionnaire (DUFSS)	I have people who care what happens to me. 5 = as much as I would like; 4 = almost as much as I would like; 3 = some, but would like more; 2 = less than I would like; 1 = much less than I would like	Broadhead et al., 1988
Perceived availability of social support and satisfaction with social support that has been received	Social Support Questionnaire	Who do you feel really appreciates you as a person?	Sarason et al., 1983
Objective: Reduce political grievances			
Attitudes toward police	Attitudes toward police	How often do think police officers physically abuse those who are accused of a crime? Is it often, sometimes, rarely, or never?	Dowler and Zawilski, 2007

Chapter Four: Evaluation Measures

**Table 4.2
Sample Outcome Measures for CVE Programs
Addressing Individuals at Risk for Violent Extremism**

Construct	Measure Name	Example Item	Reference
Public trust in government	Public trust in government	How much of the time do you think you can trust the government in [region] to do what is right? Just about always (100), most of the time (67), or only some of the time (33)?	Welch, Hinnant, and Moon, 2005
Political efficacy, political cynicism, government responsiveness, personal trust, belief in political ideals, political interest, political efficacy, citizen duty, and system evaluation	Legitimacy orientation	How much do you feel that you and your friends are well represented in our political system?	Weatherford, 1992
Objective: Improve economic conditions			
Growth and support, necessities and health, physical necessities and shelter, intrafamily support, child care, and personal resources	Family Resource Scale–Revised	To what extent are the following resources adequate for you and your family? . . . Good job for yourself or spouse.	Van Horn, Bellis, and Snyder, 2001
Personal income and Unemployment	Personal Economic Grievances	How satisfied are you with your standard of living—the things you have, like housing, car, furniture, recreation, and the like?	Kinder and Kiewiet, 1979
Objective: Improve social/economic integration			
Subjective quality of life and objective quality of life	Comprehensive Quality of Life Scale	How satisfied are you with the things you own? 7 = delighted, 6 = pleased, 5 = mostly satisfied, 4 = mixed, 3 = mostly dissatisfied, 2 = unhappy, 1 = terrible	Cummins et al., 1994

NOTE: The "Reference" column includes references to the source articles describing how the measure was developed or evaluation studies in which the measure was used.

RAND Program Evaluation Toolkit for Countering Violent Extremism

Table 4.3
Sample Outcome Measures for CVE Programs Addressing Communities That Influence Individuals at Risk for Violent Extremism

Construct	Measure Name	Example Item	Reference
Objective: Help community members understand and identify extremism and risks			
Support for violence	Support for violence	In general, I understand some extremist groups' reasons for the use of violence, even though I do not condone the violence itself.	Tausch et al., 2011
Likelihood of calling police about terrorist acts	Likelihood of calling police	How likely is it that you would call the police if you knew a person was stockpiling guns?	LaFree et al., 2013
How concerned government should be about terrorist acts	Appropriate level of government concern	How concerned should the government be if a person is distributing handouts in support of terrorism?	LaFree et al., 2013
Objective: Build capacity of community members to identify/engage with at-risk individuals			
Civic engagement	Civic engagement	[How often do you spend time] mentoring/peer advising?	Bobek et al., 2009
Sense of community	Sense of Community Index	I can recognize most of the members of this community.	Chavis, Lee, and Acosta, 2008
Perceptions of mentor	Mentorship Effectiveness Scale	My mentor was supportive and encouraging.	Berk et al., 2005
Situation-specific perceived self-efficacy: The belief that one can produce a given outcome or effectively perform a given task or role	Situation-specific perceived self-efficacy	On a scale of 0 to 100, rate how certain you are that you can [recognize the signs of individual radicalization]* Or On a scale of 0 to 100, rate how certain you are that you can effectively [engage with an individual who shows signs of radicalization]* *The self-efficacy scale allows programs to construct scales specific to the program's objectives	Bandura, 2006

62

Chapter Four: Evaluation Measures

Table 4.3
Sample Outcome Measures for CVE Programs Addressing Communities That Influence Individuals at Risk for Violent Extremism

Construct	Measure Name	Example Item	Reference
Objective: Create an environment that is accepting of minority groups			
Motivation to respond without prejudice	Internal Motivation to Respond Without Prejudice Scale (IMS) and External Motivation to Respond Without Prejudice Scale (EMS)	I am personally motivated by my beliefs to be nonprejudiced toward [black] people.	Plant and Devine, 1998
Humanitarianism	Humanitarianism-Egalitarianism Scale	One should be kind to all people.	Katz Hass, 1988
Racial/ethnic biases	Prejudicial Biases Awareness, Diffusion, and Action Questionnaire	I believe that I am able to transcend racial boundary intentions with my actions.	Lillis and Hayes, July 2007
Objective: Promote policies that address political grievances			
Political competency	Political competency	What is your ability to . . . understand the policy formulation process?	Rocha, 2000
Political activity	Political activity	How many times since graduating have you worked on a specific change effort?	Rocha, 2000
Evaluation of democracy	Evaluation of democracy	The state [or local] government respects peoples' rights.	Crow and Luskin, 2013
Objective: Strengthen government capacity to curtail violent extremism			
Cultural awareness	Cultural Awareness Scale	I think my beliefs and attitudes are influenced by my culture.	Rew et al., 2003
Police interaction perceptions	Police interaction perceptions	I have the skills necessary to interact with youth.	LaMotte et al., 2010
Strengthen government capacity to curtail violent extremism	Community perceptions of police	How would you rate the job the police are doing in terms of working with people in your neighborhood to solve neighborhood problems?	Schaefer, Huebner, and Bynum, 2003

RAND Program Evaluation Toolkit for Countering Violent Extremism

Table 4.3
Sample Outcome Measures for CVE Programs Addressing Communities That Influence Individuals at Risk for Violent Extremism

Construct	Measure Name	Example Item	Reference
Objective: Build capacity of positive and influential members and leadership to credibly counter violent extremist ideology			
Situation-specific perceived self-efficacy	Situation-specific perceived self-efficacy	On a scale of 0 to 100, please rate how certain you are that you can effectively use social media to counter racism* *The self-efficacy scale allows programs to construct scales specific to the program's objectives	Bandura, 2006
Political and civic activism	Political and civic activism	1 (not at all) to 7 (very frequently): In the past 3 months, how often have you worked on policies and issues related to [countering violent extremism]?* * This question was adapted from a measure of AIDS-related activism that involved summing results in five domains of AIDS activism. CVE programs can adapt this approach to measure CVE activism.	Omoto, Snyder, and Hackett, 2010

NOTE: The "Reference" column includes references to the source articles describing how the measure was developed or evaluation studies in which the measure was used.

Assess the Quality of Selected Measures

Use the following checklist (W. K. Kellogg Foundation, 2000) to review the information in **Template 3.1**, your draft evaluation plan. Check off each item that is true for your draft evaluation plan. The logic model (**Template 2.1**) should include the intended target population, as well as program activities and outcomes, and you should refer to it when completing this checklist.

Chapter Four: Evaluation Measures

**Checklist 4.1
To What Extent Do the Measures Selected
Align with Your Program's Target Population,
Activities, and Outcomes?**

☐ Fidelity data are linked directly to specific program activities. Refer to the program activities in your logic model.

☐ Demographic or attendance data are collected from the program participants. Refer to the target population in your logic model.

☐ Satisfaction data are collected from either the program participants or staff responsible for implementing the CVE program.

☐ Outcome data are linked directly to a specified program outcome. Refer to the logic model for program outcomes.

Summary

Nice job selecting your evaluation measures! This chapter provided information about the process and outcome measures used in prior program evaluations (**Tables 4.1** and **4.2**). After this chapter, you should have completed the "Measures" portion of your evaluation plan (**Template 3.1**) and assessed the quality of those measures (**Checklist 4.1**). Now, you're ready to start collecting data using those measures. Once you have collected the evaluation data, you can analyze the data (see technical instructions in **Appendix C**) and turn to **Chapter Five**, which will help you use your evaluation results for program improvement.

Chapter Five: Using Evaluation Data

Chapter Five
Use Evaluation Data to Improve Your Program

Objective:
To support the use of program data for continuous quality improvement.

Although it is most useful for programs that have already collected their evaluation data, this chapter can also benefit programs that are preparing to start their evaluations. This chapter begins by showing you how to assess some basic information about your program's evaluation to help you better interpret the results. This assessment is followed by a review of the evaluation findings to determine the extent to which your program achieved its intended outcomes. The chapter concludes with a series of small-scale assessments to identify appropriate changes needed to improve the quality of your program. If you have not yet analyzed the data from your evaluation, you should do that before following the steps in this chapter.

Assess Participation in Your Evaluation

Before interpreting and applying your evaluation data, revisit the final evaluation design that was actually implemented to determine how well the evaluation participants reflect the intended program participants. You will need information on who participated in the evaluation and how well that aligned with the program's intent to help inform decisions about the types of program improvements needed. Answering the questions in **Worksheet 5.1** will help you assess participation in your evaluation. Complete **Worksheet 5.1** before interpreting your evaluation data.

67

RAND Program Evaluation Toolkit for Countering Violent Extremism

Below is an example of how you might complete the worksheet:

If your program evaluation began in January 2017 and ended in August 2017, you would record this range as your period of reporting (Question A, January–August 2017). If your program intended to reach 50 civic and religious leaders in your community (Question B) and you were able to recruit 40 of those leaders to attend your program at least once (Question C), the percentage of participants reached would be 40 divided by 50 times 100 = 80 percent. If, of the 40 leaders who attended your program at least once, 36 participated in your evaluation, the percentage participating in your evaluation would be 90 percent (36/40 × 100). These two percentages will help guide your response to Question H. Because the percentage of participants reached and the percentage of that group who participated in your evaluation were both above 75 percent, your evaluation represented the intended population "very well." This suggests that you should have strong confidence in your evaluation results. Your evaluation results may not accurately describe the effectiveness of your program if they do not or only somewhat represent the intended population. Improving program recruitment and retention strategies can help ensure that you get the needed participation to accurately assess your program's effectiveness.

Chapter Five: Using Evaluation Data

Worksheet 5.1
Assessing Participation in Your Program's Evaluation
(adapted from Hunter et al., 2015)

A. What is the period of reporting?	B. How many participants did you plan to reach with your program?	C. How many attended your program even once?	D. How many people participated in the evaluation?
_____	_____	_____	_____

E. % of participants reached: _____ (number of participants who attended your program even once/number of participants you planned to reach × 100)	F. % of participants in the evaluation: _____ (number of participants in the evaluation/number of participants who attended your program even once × 100)

G. Who took part in the evaluation?
- ☐ Program completers
- ☐ Regular attendees
- ☐ Everyone who ever attended
- ☐ Others

H. How well does your evaluation represent the population you intended to reach? (Using the information above, check one.)

- ☐ **Not at all well:** This means that you did not reach the program participants you planned to reach (% of participants reached was less < 50%). It can also mean that you reached most or some of the participants you planned to reach (% of participants reached was > 50%), but few participated in the evaluation (% of participants in the evaluation was < 75%).

- ☐ **Somewhat well:** This means that you reached some of the program participants you planned to reach (% of participants reached was > 50%). Of those reached, most participated in the evaluation (% of participants in the evaluation was < 75%).

- ☐ **Very well:** This means that you reached most or all of the program participants you planned to reach (% of participants reached was > 75%), and most participated in the evaluation (% of participants in the evaluation was < 75%).

RAND Program Evaluation Toolkit for Countering Violent Extremism

Interpret the Evaluation Data

Next, we will interpret the evaluation findings by assessing whether they provide useful information about the extent to which the program achieved its intended outcomes. **Worksheet 5.3** asks you to document, through a series of questions, what types of effects the program had on each outcome and whether the program met, missed (fell short of), or exceeded expectations. Continuous quality improvement (CQI) efforts should prioritize actions directed at program outcomes where the program missed expectations. The final column in the worksheet should be used to record any barriers that may have contributed to the "missed expectation" rating. Overall, you are trying to determine whether these results suggest that changes to the program are needed.

To use this worksheet, first transfer the outcomes and associated program activities from your logic model (**Template 2.1**) to the first and second columns, respectively, of **Worksheet 5.3**. Then, record the results of your analysis (see **Appendix C**) in column 2 ("Difference/Change in Any of the Outcomes?"). Specify any changes in participants' behaviors, knowledge, skills, and so on.

Column 2 also allows you to identify trends in the results. If you did *not* see any differences in participants as a result of your program, mark that things stayed the "same." If you did see differences, specify whether these were improvements (i.e., "better") or setbacks (i.e., "worse"), based on your specified outcome. For example, if you organized a workshop to improve attitudes among a sample of youth leaders toward intervening on behalf of youth in crisis, but the results of your evaluation found that attitudes became more stigmatizing, this would be a setback and would get marked as "worse" on the worksheet.

Next, specify in column 3 ("Met Expectations?") whether these results were what you expected. Refer back to your intended outcome in column 1 to help you determine whether you achieved the results you were expecting. Building on the workshop example, if you expected that the workshop would improve attitudes and it did not, then you would check "missed" on the worksheet. Your program will need to take action to improve the outcomes for which evaluation results did not meet expectations (i.e., those marked "missed" in the third column), so mark these as "Yes" in the fourth column ("Action Needed?"). For outcomes for which action is needed, spend time reflecting on any barriers that could have kept your program from achieving that outcome and record them in the last column. **Worksheet 5.2** provides an example of how to fill out this worksheet. **Table 5.1**, discussed next, is intended to help you reflect on possible barriers.

Chapter Five: Using Evaluation Data

Worksheet 5.2
Review Program Outcomes, with Example
(adapted from Hunter et al., 2015)

Outcome	Difference/Change in Any of the Outcomes?	Met Expectations?	Action Needed?	Potential Barriers (e.g., resources, expertise)?
Example: After the parents of Beaumont High School students participate in the program for two months, their recognition of violent extremism signs and risk factors will increase by 20 percent.	15-percent increase in the Beaumont High School parents' recognition of violent extremism signs and risk factors ***Was this related to any program activities (as measured by process evaluation measures)?*** Yes, attendance data. These data showed that 65 percent of the parents participated in the full two-month program.	***What is the trend?*** ☒ Better ☐ Same ☐ Worse ***Did this meet your expectations for the program?*** ☐ Met ☒ Missed ☐ Exceeded	☒ Yes ☐ No	Parent attendance varied. May need to think about makeup sessions to accommodate parent absences.

71

RAND Program Evaluation Toolkit for Countering Violent Extremism

Worksheet 5.3
Review Program Outcomes
(based on Hunter et al., 2015)

Outcome	Difference/Change in Any of the Outcomes?		Met Expectations?	Action Needed?	Potential Barriers (e.g., resources, expertise)?
	What is the trend? ☐ Better ☐ Same ☐ Worse	Was this related to any program activities (as measured by process evaluation measures)?	Did this meet your expectations for the program? ☐ Met ☐ Missed ☐ Exceeded	☐ Yes ☐ No	
1.					

Chapter Five: Using Evaluation Data

Outcome	Difference/Change in Any of the Outcomes?	Met Expectations?	Action Needed?	Potential Barriers (e.g., resources, expertise)?
2.	*What is the trend?* ☐ Better ☐ Same ☐ Worse *Was this related to any program activities (as measured by process evaluation measures)?*	*Did this meet your expectations for the program?* ☐ Met ☐ Missed ☐ Exceeded	☐ Yes ☐ No	
3.	*What is the trend?* ☐ Better ☐ Same ☐ Worse *Was this related to any program activities (as measured by process evaluation measures)?*	*Did this meet your expectations for the program?* ☐ Met ☐ Missed ☐ Exceeded	☐ Yes ☐ No	

RAND Program Evaluation Toolkit for Countering Violent Extremism

Make a Plan to Improve Your Program

Your review of the evaluation data could suggest a number of different actions. **Table 5.1** presents a series of results-based scenarios and their associated program improvement strategies. If you indicated that the program did not meet expectations (i.e., "missed") in **Worksheet 5.3**, the program activities did not result in a significant change in intended outcomes. If you indicated that the evaluation participants did not represent the target population well (i.e., "not at all well"), the program activities were not implemented with adequate dosage or fidelity. Your process evaluation data may also help you decide whether program activities were or were not implemented with adequate dosage (i.e., participants got most or all of the intervention) and fidelity (i.e., program content was delivered as intended). Identify which scenario best describes your evaluation results and then proceed to the small-scale CQI assessments, which will help you select improvement strategies, if needed.

If changes to your program are needed, use the following CQI assessment to identify the specific changes needed and to plan key activities (see **Checklist 5.1**). The CQI assessment walks through a number of potential challenges to help you determine whether the problem is applicable to your program and then provides a description of potential actions to help address the problem. If you answer "no" to any of the questions in **Checklist 5.1**, review the associated actions and select those that your program can feasibly pursue.

Chapter Five: Using Evaluation Data

Table 5.1
Results-Based Scenarios and Associated Strategies for Program Improvement

	Program activities resulted in a significant change on intended outcomes.	
	Yes	**No**
Program activities are implemented with adequate dosage and fidelity. **Yes**	The program seems to be working as designed. Continue implementation and evaluation. • Keep monitoring process and outcomes.	*Changes may be needed* because your program did not achieve the intended results. Lack of significant results could be related to the following barriers: • A small sample size • A misalignment between program activities and intended outcomes • A mismatch between the program and its participants (e.g., participants started high on outcome measures, leaving limited room to improve) • A mismatch between evaluation design or measures and program outcomes. Address these potential barriers before implementing the program. Addressing these barriers may require you to change your program activities and your evaluation design/measures.
No	*Changes may be needed* to address potential barriers to fidelity and dosage. You might want to reevaluate the program to determine whether results improve. • Focus on strengthening areas that were not implemented with fidelity. • Improve recruiting or retention strategies to ensure that participants get an adequate dosage.	*Changes may be needed* because the program does not seem to be working as designed. Significant changes to program activities and evaluation design may be required. Assess whether • There is a mismatch between the program and the intended population • There are adequate resources to deliver the program (e.g., Do facilitators have enough training? Do participants have incentive to attend program?). Proceed to **Checklist 5.1**.

75

RAND Program Evaluation Toolkit for Countering Violent Extremism

Checklist 5.1
What CQI Actions Are Needed to Improve the Program?

A. Did participants represent your target population?

☐ Yes

☐ No ⟶ Review referral sources to determine whether you have the right relationships in place to get appropriate referrals. Review eligibility criteria to ensure that they are clear enough to recruit appropriate program participants.

B. Was the program delivered as intended?

☐ Yes

☐ No ⟶ Improve staff training on how to implement the program and self-assess fidelity.

C. Was attendance adequate?

☐ Yes

☐ No ⟶ Revisit recruitment and retention practices to identify where improvements can be made. Assess whether there are any logistical barriers that might make it difficult for participants to attend (e.g., transportation). Consider whether changing the time or place of the program would improve participation. Consider whether the program is appropriate for the population served.

D. Did you have the resources needed to implement the program completely and as intended?

☐ Yes

☐ No ⟶ Review your program's resources for implementation and evaluation to determine whether you have the right staff, resources, and partnerships to deliver the program. Try to leverage additional resources from untapped sources in your community. A community resource assessment may help inform this effort.

Chapter Five: Using Evaluation Data

Checklist 5.1
What CQI Actions Are Needed to Improve the Program?

E. Were the outcomes you expected reasonable/appropriate for the program?

☐ Yes

☐ No ⟶ Revisit the goals and logic model that you developed and revise them to be more reasonable/appropriate for your program.

F. Was your process and outcome evaluation appropriate?

☐ Yes

☐ No ⟶ Update the process and/or outcome evaluation plan to be more appropriate for your program.

Transfer to **Worksheet 5.4** the relevant improvement actions from any items in **Checklist 5.1** for which you answered "No." Then, record who will participate in the action, who will be responsible for the action, the resources needed, location details, and the target date for improvement. Making a plan for program improvement using **Worksheet 5.4** will help you identify the activities necessary to achieve those objectives and specify a target date for completing the program improvement activities. If possible, complete the program improvement activities prior to implementing the program again.

RAND Program Evaluation Toolkit for Countering Violent Extremism

Worksheet 5.4
Program Improvement Plan

Improvement Action	Who Will Participate	Who Is Responsible	Resources Needed/Source	Location/Details	Date of Completion

Chapter Five: Using Evaluation Data

Conclusion

Congratulations on completing the evaluation toolkit! We hope you found it helpful for planning and implementing an evaluation and using evaluation data for program improvement. If you skipped any steps, consider going back and completing those portions of the toolkit. Each chapter builds on information from the previous chapter:

√ **Chapter Two** helps you identify the core components of your CVE program and organize these components into a logic model. The logic model helps you clearly visualize the relationships and dependencies between components. This chapter also contains tools to help you review your logic model, assessing whether it is complete and reasonable.

√ **Chapter Three** helps you select an evaluation design that is appropriate for each of your program's core components and provides information from prior evaluations of programs that might be similar to yours.

√ **Chapter Four** helps you select process and outcome evaluation measures that are appropriate for your evaluation design and provides information from prior evaluations of programs that might be similar to yours.

√ **Chapter Five** helps you interpret the process and outcome evaluation results to guide improvements.

Fully completing each chapter will help you ensure that you have taken advantage of the comprehensive guidance provided. The content of this toolkit is intended to be used for continuous quality improvement. So, once you complete **Chapter Five** and determine whether improvements are needed, you will need to begin again at **Chapter Two** by updating your program's core components with any improvements. The content and worksheets are intended to be reused, even after you have started an evaluation or enhanced an existing evaluation. Consider reviewing the toolkit annually to continue improving your program and refining your evaluation.

Appendix A: Creating Your Own Survey

Appendix A
Creating Your Own Survey

Objective:

To provide guidance on how to develop surveys for program evaluation.

A survey can be used to assess attributes of a CVE program, including program outcomes. However, preexisting survey measures, presented in **Chapter Four**, may not be suitable for your specific CVE program. In this instance, you may need to create your own survey measures. When designing your own measures, there are several points that you should keep in mind. This appendix provides brief descriptions of several key elements in survey development.

Determine What Information You Want

Before developing your own survey, you should first determine what you want to measure. Important questions to answer before creating your survey include the following (Diem, 2002):

- What information do I need to know?
- Why do I need to know this information?
- What will happen as a result of the information I collect using this survey?

To evaluate the quality of your program, you may want to measure certain program outputs, or *process measures*. In **Template 2.1** in **Chapter Two**, you identified outputs in your logic model. Some outputs, such as participant satisfaction and other participant perceptions of the program, can be assessed using a survey. You can also survey program staff on their perceptions of the program.

To evaluate program impact, you should identify the specific outcomes that you expect to see. Review the outcome measures you identified in your logic model. Examples include the following (Barkman, 2002):

RAND Program Evaluation Toolkit for Countering Violent Extremism

- Awareness of particular programs or social issues
- Knowledge of certain topics addressed in the program
- Attitudes regarding certain groups or behaviors
- Intentions to engage in specific social actions.

Determine When You Want to Administer the Survey

You will also need to determine when to administer the survey. Ideally, you will administer the survey both immediately before and immediately after your intervention. In this way, you can determine whether the intervention led to changes in key outcome measures. You can also administer the survey as a follow-up measure. For example, you might ask participants to complete the survey several months or more after the intervention to determine whether post-intervention changes were sustained. Remember that it is important to be consistent in how you word the questions and response options when administering a survey across different time points.

Decide Whom to Survey

Next, you need to determine whom you will survey. As noted, you can survey program staff as a process measure, or you can survey participants. If you intend to survey program participants, you should determine whether you want to survey the entire participant population or whether you want to obtain information from a subsample.

If your program is relatively small, it might make sense to survey all program participants. If your program is large (e.g., several thousand or more), then you can survey a subsample (Salant and Dillman, 1994). When developing the subsample, you should determine a sample size and method of sampling that ensures that your sample is representative of the participant population. In other words, your sample should represent the characteristics of all individuals in the population. If those who respond to your survey are very different from those who do not respond, then the results of your survey may be questionable. Specifically, you will not be able to determine whether the survey results are representative of all program participants' perceptions and behaviors or whether the results are unusual due to responses from a unique subset of participants.

Tailor Survey Vocabulary to Your Audience

Adapt the wording of survey questions to correspond to the vocabulary and reading abilities of those you intend to survey (Dillman, Smyth, and Christina, 2009). **Table A.1** suggests some alternatives for commonly used concepts. Avoid the use of abbreviations, acronyms, or jargon that may confuse those who take your survey.

Appendix A: Creating Your Own Survey

Table A.1
Use Simple Words and Phrases

Complex Words and Phrases		Simplified Words and Phrases
Rectify	→	Correct
Candid	→	Honest
Leisure	→	Free time
Post-school extracurricular activities	→	What you do after school
What is the frequency. . . ?	→	How many times. . . ?

Write High-Quality Questions That Address What You Want to Know

Structure survey questions and response options in ways that allow participants to easily understand and respond to the questions. Consider whether participants will be able to understand and respond to the questions, whether the questions will provide credible information, and whether participants will feel comfortable responding to the questions (Salant and Dillman, 1994).

Use Clear and Concise Question Wording

Wording of questions should be concise and unambiguous. Each question should address only one concept at a time. Poorly written survey questions include those that address more than one concept but require participants to provide a single answer. These questions are known as double-barreled questions, and they should be avoided (DeVellis, 2012).

Example of a double-barreled question:

To what extent did your teacher provide useful information and address your questions?

In the above question, a teacher's provision of useful information and the extent to which the teacher addressed questions are two separate topics. These two topics should be addressed in separate questions. Often, the use of "and" in can be indicative of a double-barreled question.

Addressing the above double-barreled question:

To what extent did your teacher provide useful information?
To what extent did your teacher address your questions?

The two questions above each address one topic each. Therefore, it will be clear which topic participants are considering in their responses.

RAND Program Evaluation Toolkit for Countering Violent Extremism

Avoid lengthy questions that include unnecessary details. Overly wordy questions may confuse participants or lead them to lose interest in completing the survey question (Chavez, 2016).

Example wordy question:
During an average week in January 2017, what amount of time, in hours, did you devote to preparing for the next workshop, whether by reading workshop material, reviewing notes from previous workshops, talking with other workshop participants, or talking with colleagues or community members?

The above question is lengthy and contains multiple unnecessary details that may confuse participants or cause to them skipping the question entirely.

Addressing the above wordy question:
In a typical week in January 2017, how many hours did you spend preparing for a workshop?

The above question captures the information desired in a clear and concise manner.

Phrase questions in a way that ensures that every participant has a similar understanding of the question's meaning and intent (DeVellis, 2012). Further, in questions involving a period of time, you should be specific about the exact period of interest. Questions that are interpreted in different ways by different participants can lead to ambiguous results.

Example ambiguous question:
How often have you seen someone about your health in the past few months?

In the above question, it is not clear what type of health practitioner is of interest to survey administrators. Participants may respond to this question by only referencing professionals with a medical degree, or they may also include family members and friends as individuals whom they have seen about their health. Further, it is not clear whether this question is addressing physical health, psychological health, or both. Finally, the time period of interest is also ambiguous, so some participants may interpret a few months as indicative of three months, and others may consider more than three months to be indicative of a "few" months.

Addressing the above ambiguous question:
From January 2016 through June 2016, how many times did you see a psychiatrist or psychologist?

The above question reduces ambiguity in the time frame and type of health practitioner of interest.

Appendix A: Creating Your Own Survey

Eliminate Biased Wording

Avoid leading questions that prompt participants to respond in a certain way. Ensure that questions are worded in a way that accommodates different opinions or responses (e.g., positive and negative) (Dillman, Smyth, and Christina, 2009).

Example leading question:
Previous participants found this workshop to be highly informative. How informative did you find this workshop?

The above question biases participants to respond favorably. It reduces the likelihood that participants' who did not find the workshop informative will provide an honest response.

Addressing the above leading question:
How informative or uninformative did you find this workshop?

The above question is written in a neutral manner that allows participants to provide honest feedback. It considers both positive (i.e., informative) and negative (i.e., uninformative) opinions of the workshop.

Consider Whether and How to Address Sensitive Topics

Questions that address sensitive topics may lead participants to feel uncomfortable or alienated. Participants may provide dishonest responses or skip questions that ask for highly sensitive information. You should avoid asking sensitive questions to obtain information that is not crucial to your program (Crano and Brewer, 2002). Certain sensitive questions, such as demographic questions (e.g., income, age, education level), may be necessary. Place sensitive questions near the end of a survey and include an option that allows participants to refuse to provide a response (e.g., "Decline to answer") (Chavez, 2016).

Determine Appropriate Question Structure

Different question structures may be used in a survey. Four common structures are open-ended, close-ended with ordered choices, closed-ended with unordered choices, and partially close-ended (Salant and Dillman, 1994). Each question structure is suited for obtaining a different type of information.

Open-Ended

Example open-ended question:

What specific issues are you interested in related to countering violent extremism in the United States?

RAND Program Evaluation Toolkit for Countering Violent Extremism

Rather than providing participants with a limited number of response options, open-ended questions require that participants formulate their own response. Open-ended questions can provide participants with a chance to describe strong opinions, and these questions are useful when there is insufficient information regarding a question topic to provide specific response options. However, these questions demand more time and effort of participants than close-ended options. In addition, different participants will answer an open-ended question in different ways and may not mention the same topics or information. This can make the question difficult to analyze and summarize. The use of open-ended questions also demands more time and effort on the part of the program administrator or evaluator. It takes more time to review participant responses, and it is more difficult to use these responses to systematically measure impact.

Close-Ended with Ordered Choices

Example closed-ended question with ordered choices:

How do you feel about this statement? "This community needs more police involvement."

1. Strongly disagree
2. Mildly disagree
3. Neither agree nor disagree
4. Mildly agree
5. Strongly agree

Close-ended questions with ordered choices provide participants with a complete range of possible answers to a question. Using the available response options, participants indicate which option best fits their opinion or characteristic. These questions require little effort for participants to complete and may be easier for administrators to analyze and summarize than open-ended questions. When providing ordered response options, you should arrange the options in a logical order (e.g., strongly disagree to strongly agree) and maintain this order for all questions with these response options throughout the survey.

Close-Ended with Unordered Choices

Example closed-ended question with unordered choices:

From which one of these sources did you first hear about this program?

• Radio
• Television
• Internet
• Newspaper
• Another person

Closed-ended questions with unordered choices provide response options that do not have a clearly identifiable order. This type of question should be used only when you can provide participants with a complete list of useful response options. If participants have an answer that is not captured by the available response options, they will not be able to complete the question accurately. These types of questions may be more difficult for participants to complete than closed-ended questions with ordered choices, as participants must carefully consider each option before responding.

Partially Closed-Ended

Example partially closed-ended question:

From which one of these sources did you first hear about this program?

- Radio
- Television
- Internet
- Newspaper
- Another person
- Other (describe): _____

Partially closed-ended questions provide participants with specific answer choices but also allow participants to create their own response option. Partially closed-ended questions tend to involve the use of unordered response options, with the addition of a final open-ended response option.

Address Survey Structure

In addition to the wording and structure of individual questions, you should also carefully consider the design of the overall survey. Surveys that are not well organized can confuse and frustrate participants, leading them to discontinue survey participation.

Provide a Survey Introduction

Before launching into your survey questions, you should provide a short introduction to the survey. In this introduction, you should briefly describe the topics that are addressed and explain how the survey results will be used. This information can encourage individuals to complete the survey.

Keep the Survey Short and Well Organized

When creating a survey, you should avoid asking questions that you are unlikely to use to inform your program. By keeping a survey shorter, you will reduce the burden on participants to complete the survey, and they will be more likely to participate (Dillman, Smyth, and Christina, 2009). In addition, you should order questions in a logical way, such as by grouping together questions that address the same or similar topics. As mentioned previously, any questions addressing sensitive topics and demographics should be placed at the end of the survey; begin the survey with questions that are easier to answer and more impersonal (Chavez, 2016).

Say Thank You

At the conclusion of a survey, you should thank individuals for their participation and provide contact information that they may use to follow up with possible questions or concerns. This demonstrates positive regard for participants.

RAND Program Evaluation Toolkit for Countering Violent Extremism

Pretesting the Survey

After creating your survey, you should have a small group of individuals similar to those in your participant population review the survey's questions and response options. You can ask these individuals to provide you with recommendations regarding how to improve the wording and structure of the survey questions (Willis, 1999). These individuals can also provide suggestions regarding topics that appear to be missing from the survey or unnecessary topics that are addressed.

Surveys that are hastily created can produce results that lack credibility and utility. By carefully considering whom you would like to complete your survey, your question wording and format, and your survey structure, you can create and administer a survey that is likely to provide high-quality and useful results.

Appendix A: Creating Your Own Survey

Worksheet A.1
Steps for Creating an Assessment Survey

Use this worksheet to help you design and structure a survey for program evaluation. Use the following questions to help you create your own questions; when possible, you should use questions and scales that have already been validated and published.

Step 1: What Do You Need to Know?

Step 1 Instructions: Respond to the questions below to address what topics may be of interest for your survey.

1. *Reactions:* Reactions involve how participants *feel* about different aspects of a program. Do you want to know how participants feel about different aspects of your program?

☐ No ⟶ Skip to Question 2

☐ Yes ⟶ Possible questions could address overall performance of a speaker/leader, the usefulness of a subject, and level of satisfaction with the information provided. Complete the table below to develop questions about participant reactions.

Participant Reaction Write program characteristics on which you would like to receive feedback. Use a separate box for each characteristic.	Proposed Question Write a survey question that addresses what you wrote in the leftmost column.	Response Format Write the survey response options that you would like participants to use to respond to the question in the middle column.

RAND Program Evaluation Toolkit for Countering Violent Extremism

Worksheet A.1
Steps for Creating an Assessment Survey

2. *Learning:* Refers to knowledge, skills, or attitudes that improved or changed as a result of program participation. Do you want to know whether/how participants' knowledge, skills, or attitudes improved or changed as a result of your program?

☐ No ⟶ Skip to Question 3

☐ Yes ⟶ Measuring actual changes in participants' knowledge, skills, or attitudes can require somewhat complex research methods. A simpler approach may involve collecting data from one group at one time: Rather than administering more than one survey to detect changes in knowledge, skills, or attitudes, you might consider simply asking participants whether they think their knowledge, skills, or attitudes changed as a result of the program. Complete the table below to develop questions about knowledge, skills, and attitudes.

Participant Knowledge, Attitudes, or Skills Write what topic knowledge, skill, or attitude you expect your program to change. Use a separate box for each point.	Proposed Question Write a survey question that addresses the point you wrote in the leftmost column. Consider asking about perceived changes.	Response Format Write the survey response options that you would like participants to use to respond to the question in the middle column.

Appendix A: Creating Your Own Survey

Worksheet A.1
Steps for Creating an Assessment Survey

---

3. *Behavior:* Behaviors involve the extent to which participants change their behavior as a result of a program. Do you want to know how participants change their behavior as a result of your program?

☐ No ⟶ Skip to Question 4

☐ Yes ⟶ Measuring actual changes in behavior can require somewhat complex research methods. A simpler approach may involve collecting data from one group at one time: Rather than administering more than one survey to detect changes in behavior, you might consider simply asking participants whether they intend to change their behavior. Complete the table below to develop questions about intentions to change behaviors.[1]

Participant Behavior Write down the participant behaviors that you expect your program to change. Use a separate box for each behavior.	Proposed Question Write a survey question that addresses the behavior that you wrote in the leftmost column. Consider asking about intentions to change the behavior.	Response Format Write the survey response options that you would like participants to use to respond to the question in the middle column.

---

[1] Questions about intended behavior changes are best asked immediately after an intervention, when participants may be motivated to change their behavior but have not yet had an opportunity to do so. If the survey will have a follow-up component (e.g., administered weeks or months after the intervention), then it may also be possible to ask about the frequency with which participants engage in a behavior of interest (i.e., "How frequently have you posted antiradicalization content on social media?" Daily, 3–4 times per week; 1–2 times per week; 1–3 times per month; not at all).

RAND Program Evaluation Toolkit for Countering Violent Extremism

Worksheet A.1
Steps for Creating an Assessment Survey

4. *Open-ended feedback questions:* Sometimes, it is helpful to give participants an opportunity to provide unstructured feedback on the quality of the program or to provide suggestions for program improvement. Do you want to ask participants to provide comments on program quality or improvements?

☐ No ⟶ Skip to Step 2

☐ Yes ⟶ Document your questions here and provide a space for participants to respond. Remember that systematically analyzing responses to these questions can be difficult if you have a large data set, so it is best to limit the number of such questions, keep them focused on program feedback, and avoid using these questions to assess outcome.

Open-Ended Feedback Question(s)

_____
_____
_____
_____
_____
_____
_____
_____
_____

Appendix A: Creating Your Own Survey

Worksheet A.1
Steps for Creating an Assessment Survey

5. *Participant Characteristics:* Participant characteristics include information about who participated in your program. Most programs want at least a little information about who participated. Do you want to know about participant characteristics?

☐ No ⟶ Skip to Step 2

☐ Yes ⟶ Questions could ask about such characteristics as age, gender, and profession. Complete the table below to develop questions about participant characteristics.

Participant Characteristic Write down the participant characteristics of interest to your program. Use a separate box for each characteristic.	Proposed Question Write a survey question that addresses the characteristic in the leftmost column.	Response Format Write the survey response options that you would like participants to use to respond to the question in the middle column.

If none of the topics listed in Step 1 is of interest to your program, a survey may not be appropriate at this time. If some of the topics listed in Step 1 are of interest and you have drafted questions for those topics, proceed to Step 2.

RAND Program Evaluation Toolkit for Countering Violent Extremism

Worksheet A.1
Steps for Creating an Assessment Survey

Step 2: Are Your Questions Clear and Concise?

Step 2 Instructions: For each of [the survey questions you wrote in Step 1, respond to the following questions.

Question
Use tailored vocabulary: Are the question's words and phrases simple?
Avoid double-barreled questions: Are you addressing only one topic per question?
Avoid ambiguity: Is it clear who, what, and (if appropriate) what time frame your question is addressing?
Avoid leading: Are your questions worded in a way that addresses different potential opinions or responses (e.g., positive and negative)?
Ask for crucial information: Is this question crucial to your program?

If you answered "No" to any of the above questions, reword your question or eliminate it entirely. When you can respond "Yes" to all of the above for all of the questions that you have written, proceed to Step 3.

Step 3: Are Your Questions' Response Options Appropriate?

Step 3 Instructions: For the response options for each of the survey questions you wrote in Step 1, respond to the following questions.

Response Options
Do your response options reflect how participants might want to respond?
Will the response options yield information in a format that you can use to understand your program?

If you answered "No" to either of the above questions, restructure your response options. When you can respond "Yes" to both for all of the response options that you have written, proceed to Step 4.

Appendix A: Creating Your Own Survey

Worksheet A.1
Steps for Creating an Assessment Survey

Step 4: How Do You Want to Introduce Your Survey?

Step 4 Instructions: Before providing participants with a list of survey questions, you should provide a short introduction to the survey that briefly describes the topics that are addressed and explains how the survey results will be used. In the space below, write a short survey introduction. Once you have written a survey introduction, proceed to Step 5.

Survey Introduction

_____
_____
_____
_____
_____
_____
_____

Step 5: How Do You Want to End Your Survey?

Step 5 Instructions: At the conclusion of a survey, you should thank individuals for their participation and provide contact information that they may use to follow up with questions or concerns. Write a brief thank-you and provide information that participants can use to contact survey administrators below. Once you have written a survey conclusion, proceed to Step 6.

Survey Conclusion

_____
_____
_____
_____
_____
_____
_____

RAND Program Evaluation Toolkit for Countering Violent Extremism

Worksheet A.1
Steps for Creating an Assessment Survey

Step 6: Structure Your Survey

Step 6 Instructions: You are now ready to structure your survey. First, begin with the introduction you wrote in Step 4. Next, group the questions that you wrote in Step 1 in a logical order—for example, group together questions that address the same or similar topics. Finally, finish your survey with the conclusion that you wrote in Step 5.

Step 7: Pretest Your Survey

Step 7 Instructions: Have a small group of individuals who are similar to your participants (e.g., in terms of age, education level) review the questions and response options in your survey. For each of your survey questions, ask this small group of individuals to respond to the questions below.

Pretest Each Question
Is there a better way to word this question? If so, how could the wording be changed?
Are the response options for this question appropriate? If not, how would you change them?
Is the topic that this question addresses appropriate? If not, should this question be changed or removed?

For the survey as a whole, also ask the small group of individuals to respond to the questions below.

Pretest Survey
Are there any topics that are not addressed in this survey but should be? If so, what are the missing topics?
Is the survey an appropriate length or not?

Appendix A: Creating Your Own Survey

Summary

Congratulations! You have now developed a survey that you can use to better understand participants' responses to your program and its potential impact.

Depending on the suitability of measures identified in **Chapter Four**, it may be necessary for you to draft your own survey. This appendix provided brief descriptions of several key elements of survey development that will be important for you to consider. Surveys can consists of open-ended questions, close-ended questions with ordered or unordered choices, and partially closed-ended questions. In developing your survey, it will be important for you to consider the type of information you want to collect, the times you want to administer the survey, and the participants you want to survey. In crafting a survey, it is important to draft questions that are clear and concise, avoid biased wording, and carefully address sensitive topics. If possible, pretest your survey with a small group of individuals and use this input to make final improvements before your evaluation. This appendix also provided a worksheet to guide you through survey development.

Appendix B: Social Media Metrics

Appendix B
Social Media Metrics

Objective:

To identify the available metrics for social media–based programming.

Many programs use social media to help counter violent extremism or publicize CVE programs (Kaplan and Haenlein, 2010). Information, or metrics, available through various social media platforms can provide useful information regarding program outputs and outcomes. Below, we describe several social media metrics that CVE programs may use to inform their efforts. Because the social media landscape is constantly changing, we offer only a sample of potential metrics and do not attempt to comprehensively cover all available or potential metrics. We recommend reviewing guides from the different social media applications for the most up-to-date information on available metrics. *PC Magazine* also publishes information about social media metrics, and peer-reviewed journals frequently publish articles on the use of these metrics (see, for example, *Journalism and Mass Communication, Computers in Human Behavior,* and the *Journal of Interactive Marketing*).

Social Networking Sites

Social networking sites use applications that allow users to interact with each other by creating profiles that contain personal and other information and by sharing information with other users (Kaplan and Haenlein, 2010).

Facebook

Facebook allows users to post status updates, share various types of content (e.g., pictures, videos, hyperlinks), share other users' posts, send private messages to one another, and create Facebook-based web pages for their organization or event. Users can respond to a Facebook post or page by writing a comment, "liking" it (i.e., indicating support), or selecting one of a series of emoticons

RAND Program Evaluation Toolkit for Countering Violent Extremism

(e.g., angry, surprised). Different Facebook metrics are available to users, depending on which functions or services users implement. Most Facebook metrics are available only to those who advertise on the site or create a Facebook page for their organization, business, or service.

Metrics

As noted, organizations and businesses can create their own Facebook pages that contain information about organization characteristics, services, or events. Currently available Facebook performance metrics for these pages include the following information on page performance ("Page Insights"):

- *Total page reach:* The number of users who engaged with a Facebook page or viewed any activity on the page (e.g., posts made by page administrators, posts to a page by other people, page likes, page mentions)
- *Post reach:* The total number of users who viewed a post on a Facebook page
- *Total page likes:* The total number of "likes" a Facebook page has received
- *Page net likes:* The number of "likes" a Facebook page has received minus the number of "unlikes" the page has received
- *Page mentions:* The number of times a Facebook page was mentioned in user posts
- *People engaged:* The users who have liked, commented on, or shared a Facebook page's posts or engaged with a Facebook page in the past 28 days.

In addition to posting content on individual Facebook profiles, users can disseminate content via Facebook targeted advertising or Facebook pages. Advertisers can profile the recipients of their ads by specifying desired audience characteristics, including age, gender, location, language, and interests (Kapp, Peters, and Oliver, 2013). Facebook's Ads Manager application helps users assess the impact of this advertising. The metrics frequently change, but recently provided advertising performance metrics in Ads Manager include the following:

- *Frequency:* The average number of times an advertisement was shown to Facebook users
- *Reach:* The total number of Facebook users who were shown an advertisement
- *Impressions:* The number of times an advertisement appeared on Facebook users' screens for the first time
- *Results:* The total number of actions (e.g., website clicks) taken as a result of an advertisement
- *Clicks (all):* The total number of times an advertisement has been clicked on
- *Link clicks:* The number of times users clicked on links in an advertisement (e.g., links to other websites)
- *Cost per click:* The advertising cost per user who clicked on the ad.

Appendix B: Social Media Metrics

Twitter

Twitter is a free social networking application that allows users to send and receive short messages (no more than 140 characters) called tweets. Registered Twitter users can both send and receive tweets, follow other users, and accrue followers who directly receive the user's tweets. Followers can repost a registered user's tweet in their own Twitter feed. Follows can also favorite a tweet, which indicates their support for or interest in that tweet. This interaction between Twitter users provides a rich source of metrics data.

Metrics

Twitter's Activity Dashboard provides data on a user's tweet performance. Twitter's Audience Insights Dashboard provides information on users who follow these entities. This information can help CVE programs better assess the reach of their Twitter broadcasts and their engagement with audiences. As with Facebook, the metrics indicate changes over time. Below, we list several recent metrics available on these dashboards.

- *Activity Dashboard:* A tool that provides information on the performance of a user's tweets. Several pieces of information are included in this dashboard:
  - *Total impressions:* The total number of times Twitter users saw any of a user's tweets over the past 28 days
  - *Impressions:* The number of times users saw a particular tweet while using Twitter
  - *Engagements:* The sum of four ways in which users can interact with a tweet, which include the following:
    - ◦ *Replies:* The number of times other users referenced a tweet in their own posts
    - ◦ *Retweets:* The number of times other users reposted or shared a tweet to their own Twitter accounts
    - ◦ *Mentions:* The number of times other users referenced the Twitter account in tweets they posted to their own feeds
    - ◦ *Favorites (or "likes"):* The number of times other users favorited, or indicated support for, a tweet.
  - *Engagement rate:* The number of engagements (sum of replies, retweets, mentions, and favorites) divided by the number of impressions.
- *Audience Insights Dashboard:* A tool that provides information on a Twitter user's followers. In certain cases, Twitter also provides information on all Twitter users and organic audiences (i.e., on the account's Twitter followers and the number of Twitter users who see content from an account). CVE programs can use this information to better understand target audiences that engage with the program's Twitter account and better tailor content to that audience. The dashboard includes several pieces of information:
  - *Followers:* The total number of individuals who follow an account or an account's audience
  - *Interests:* The proportion of an account's followers who have indicated an interest in certain types of content (e.g., business and news, politics and current events)
  - *Occupation:* The proportion of an account's followers who hold certain types of occupations (e.g., student, management)
  - *Gender:* The proportion of an account's followers who are male and the proportion who are female (note that these statistics are not necessarily supplied to Twitter by users)

RAND Program Evaluation Toolkit for Countering Violent Extremism

- *Household income:* The proportion of an account's followers who are in certain income categories (e.g., $25,000–$49,999; note that these statistics are not necessarily supplied to Twitter by users)
- *Marital status:* The proportion of an account's followers who have different marital statuses (e.g., single, married; note that these statistics are not necessarily supplied to Twitter by users)
- *Country:* The proportion of an account's followers who live in certain countries.

Google+

Google+ is a free social networking site that allows users to post messages to share with the public or certain groups or to create Google+ web pages for their organization or company.

Google Analytics is a free Google service that provides information about Google+ profile performance. This information is updated frequently. Several pieces of information recently collected on Google+ profiles are listed below. This information can be segmented in various ways (e.g., by continent, country, city, date range, age, gender).

- *Sessions:* Total number of times users have actively engaged with a Google+ page
- *Users:* Total number of Google+ users who have had at least one session with a Google+ page
- *Page views:* Total number of times a Google+ page has been viewed; repeated views by a single Google+ user are counted multiple times
- *Average session duration:* The average length of time users are actively engaged with a Google+ page
- *Bounce rate:* Percentage of times a Google+ user visited a Google+ page without interacting with it (e.g., clicking on links).

Blogs

A blog is a personal online journal that is frequently updated and intended for general public consumption (WhatIs.com, undated). A variety of different platforms, including WordPress and Squarespace, host blogs, so available analytics can vary. We describe several metrics below with the acknowledgment that this is not a comprehensive review. These metrics can help bloggers identify their most active blog posts, sites that refer individuals to the blog, and the characteristics of users who visit the blog. For CVE programs that utilize blogs, this information can assist in evaluating blog efficacy and, subsequently, making informed modifications to better meet the blog's intended goals.

Well-known blog metrics include the following:

- *Page views:* Total number of times a blog has been viewed; repeated views by a single individual are counted multiple times
- *Traffic sources:* The number of individuals referred to a blog from other web pages; can include traffic from search engines and visitors who directly entered the blog's URL.
- *Average time on site:* The average amount of time that individuals spend viewing a particular blog's content

Appendix B: Social Media Metrics

- *Goal conversion:* Using a blogger-specified goal, this metric provides information on the number and proportion of visitors who met the criterion (for example, the number of visitors who clicked on a particular URL, such as a registration or contact page)
- *Visitor frequency:* The number of times individuals visited the blog.

The number and content of comments on blog posts can also provide information about a blog's audience.

YouTube

YouTube is a free video-hosting platform that allows members to store and share video content. YouTube users can host a homepage, called a YouTube channel, which serves as a landing page for their uploaded video content, and other users can subscribe to that page.

Google, which owns YouTube, provides a Creator Studio Dashboard with analytics for YouTube channels and individual videos. Several core YouTube metrics are as follows:

- *Video views:* The number of times a video or set of videos on a YouTube channel was viewed during a specific time period
- *Demographics:* Video views segmented by viewer gender, country, and age
- *Average view duration:* The number of minutes users spent watching videos from a YouTube channel
- *Engagement*
  - *Likes:* The number of likes (i.e., thumbs up) a video or set of videos from a specific YouTube channel has received
  - *Dislikes:* The number of dislikes (i.e., thumbs down) a video or set of videos from a specific YouTube channel has received
  - *Comments:* The number of comments a video or set of videos from a specific YouTube channel has received
  - *Subscribers:* The number of people who have subscribed or unsubscribed to a YouTube channel.

Summary

Across social media platforms, there are hundreds—if not thousands—of potential metrics that CVE programs can use to better understand their audience and evaluate the effectiveness of their social media campaigns. Facebook, Twitter, and Google+ are three of the best-known social networking sites, and each provides its own set of metrics for analyzing audience characteristics. Blogs and YouTube are additional avenues for social media that also have multiple analytic options. The specific metrics that a CVE program uses will depend on its social media content and the goals associated with posting this information.

Appendix C: Analyzing Evaluation Data

Appendix C

Analyze Your Program's Evaluation Data

Objective:

To explain how to enter and analyze the evaluation data collected about your program.

This appendix begins by summarizing how to develop a database that will allow you to link process and outcome measures over time. Then, we review three simple procedures to ensure the accuracy of the evaluation data. The appendix concludes with three primers that provide step-by-step instructions for analyzing evaluation data at an intermediate and more advanced level using Microsoft Excel® (version 2007 or later). The three primers are meant to be referenced after you have collected your evaluation data and are ready to begin analysis. If you have not yet completed data collection as part of your evaluation, you can still review the beginning of this appendix to help prepare for data analysis. Users who are unfamiliar with statistical analysis may also wish to consult a statistician rather than trying to analyze their own program evaluation data.

How to Use This Appendix

The chapter provides guidance on how to

1. Create an evaluation database
2. Decide how to analyze your evaluation data
3. Analyze data using Microsoft Excel (version 2007 or later).

Your approach to the evaluation database and analysis will vary depending on the type of evaluation you are performing. If you are using any type of pre/post design (typical, retrospective, or with a comparison or control group), you will want to be able to link a program participant's score on the pretest with his or her score on the

RAND Program Evaluation Toolkit for Countering Violent Extremism

post-test. Instructions for how to link these scores and enter them into a database for analysis are provided in the following section.

Establish an Evaluation Database

An evaluation database should contain rows and columns of data. Each row should represent a different program participant, and the columns should represent different variables collected on each participant. If you are using a control or comparison group, you should also create a column that labels each participant as belonging to the control/comparison (e.g., =0) or intervention (e.g., =1) group. Your evaluation database should contain unique identifiers for each participant, rather than participant names. These unique identifiers replace names and are needed to ensure that your program does not compromise participants' confidentiality. Names should be separated before storing or entering any data into the database. If you are collecting process or outcome data that contain participant names or other potentially identifying information, the data will need to be stored securely (e.g., in a locked file cabinet) so that others cannot access this information.

Unique Identifiers

To ensure that you can link process and outcome evaluation data, you will need to first assign unique identifiers to all program participants. A unique identifier is usually a numerical code that identifies each participant without the use of names or other identifying information. An easy way to do this is to create a prefilled template with numerical codes that can be assigned to specific participants by program staff.

Figure C.1 shows a dosage log or attendance sheet that program staff can use to record the name of each participant next to the numerical code that serves as the unique identifier. Once the program is over, the participant names can be removed and kept in a single location to ensure data security. Data analysis can then proceed using only the code numbers.

The process evaluation data can then be linked to outcome data by program staff prior to collection. For example, if you are conducting a pre/post survey, consider the example in **Figure C.2**. On the first page of the survey form (tear-off sheet), enter the participants' name and unique identifier and indicate whether the survey is the pre- or post-test. Repeating the code number on the second page of the survey. In this way, you can link specific codes with participant surveys but easily separate the names of the survey participants. The code number in the example is the number next to the participant's name on the attendance sheet (e.g., 6101, 7238).

Accurate Data Entry

Three procedures can greatly improve the accuracy of data entry. First, establish ranges or data types (see **Figure C.3**). For example, in Excel, you can specify whether the information entered is a number, date, text string, or another type, and you can limit the range of data entered (e.g., entries must be between 1 and 4). Setting up these parameters can help staff minimize data-entry errors.

106

Appendix C: Analyzing Evaluation Data

Figure C.1
Sample Attendance Sheet with Unique Identifiers

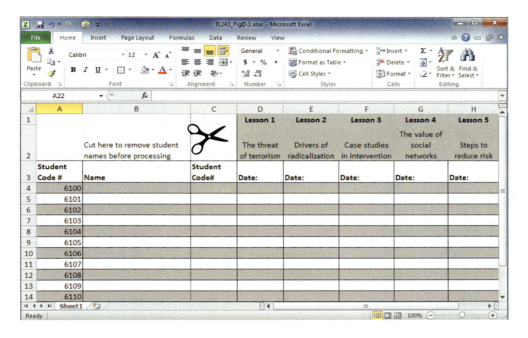

Figure C.2
Survey Cover Sheet with Unique Identifier

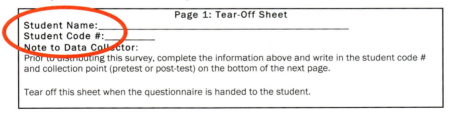

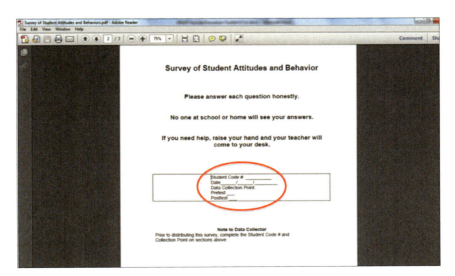

Figure C.3
Formatting Ranges in Excel

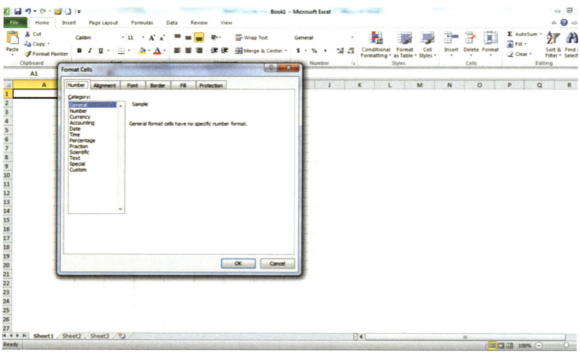

Second, have two people assigned to data entry. The first person should be responsible for entering the data, and the second person should be responsible for reviewing the data entered. Third, have a supervisor spot-check 10–25 percent of entries on an ongoing basis. If errors appear, share these errors with the data-entry staff and develop a plan to prevent similar errors or inconsistencies in the future.

Analyze Evaluation Data

There are many ways to analyze your evaluation data. We summarize three options here: (1) using Excel for basic analyses, (2) using a statistical software package, and (3) hiring an external evaluator to conduct the analyses.

Microsoft Excel can be used to conduct some basic descriptive analyses (e.g., summarize participant characteristics); to analyze pre- and post-test data to see whether program participants' attitudes, knowledge, skills, or behaviors, change; and to determine whether program participants' attendance, satisfaction, or other characteristics contributed to changes in their attitudes, knowledge, skills, or behaviors.

There are statistical packages that help automate many analysis functions. These statistical packages are efficient ways to analyze data, but they require some level of user proficiency and familiarity with statistical jargon. Another way to analyze evaluation data is to hire an external evaluator with expertise in data analysis and access to statistical software. While costs are involved for both of these options, your analysis can be done more efficiently. An external

Appendix C: Analyzing Evaluation Data

evaluator can also provide the expertise to ensure that the data analysis is executed appropriately and that it accurately reflects program outcomes. Statistical packages afford other advantages, like being able to conduct interrupted time-series analyses that are likely to be very useful for programs that collect data over time. The American Evaluation Association provides a searchable database of members available for evaluation consulting (see the references list at the end of this toolkit for a link to its "Find an Evaluator" database).

If you have not yet completed data collection for your evaluation, we suggest that you return to the primers presented in this appendix once you have collected your evaluation data.

Using Excel to Analyze Data

To facilitate access to low-cost analysis options, we provide three analysis primers that describe how to use Excel 2010 to conduct descriptive analyses, run statistical models for detecting differences in your program's target population, and link process and outcome data. These primers range from basic (i.e., descriptive analyses) to more advanced (i.e., statistical models for detecting differences). All three primers were designed to be used with Microsoft Excel 2010, so the examples provide instructions specific to this version of the application. We selected Excel because it is a common and basic processing program. Before selecting a primer for your analysis, consider the types of questions you want to ask. You may not need to use all the primers, so refer to **Table C.1** to make a decision about your data analysis goals and which primer(s) will be most useful to you.

Before you use these primers to analyze data, you will need to enable the "Data Analysis" function in Excel. To do this, go to the data tab at the top of the Excel screen. If you do not see a button labeled "Data Analysis," you will have to complete the following procedure:

1. Left-click on the green tab marked "File" at the top left of the screen, then select "Options."
2. In the left panel, click the "Add-Ins" button. At the bottom of the screen in the right panel next to "Manage," make sure that "Excel Add-Ins" is selected. Then press "Go."
3. A new window will open; ensure that both "Analysis ToolPak" options are checked and then click "OK."
4. When you return to the data tab you should see a button called "Data Analysis."

Table C.1
Types of Analyses Addressed in
Each Data Analysis Primer

Primers in This Chapter	Uses for Each Primer
Primer 1: Calculating Descriptive Statistics for Your Program	Describe the key characteristics of program participants
	Summarize attendance
	Describe participant satisfaction
	Calculate averages and other descriptive data (e.g., percentages, frequencies, ranges, modes) for each outcome variable
Primer 2: Statistical Models for Detecting Differences in Your Program's Target Population	Analyze pre- and post-test data to see whether program participants' knowledge, skills, or behaviors change (e.g., Does the program achieve its outcomes?)
Primer 3: Linking Process to Outcome Measures	Determine whether program participants' attendance, satisfaction, or other characteristics contributed to changes in their knowledge, skills, or behaviors

Appendix C: Analyzing Evaluation Data

Primer 1: Calculating Descriptive Statistics for Your Program

In this primer, we review how to calculate some basic descriptive statistics on your program. In your evaluation database, you are likely to have three types of variables: dichotomous, continuous, and categorical. The first step of any analysis is to determine what type of variables you have.

- *Continuous variables* are those for which there are multiple outcomes along a continuum—for example, age or height. Sometimes, there is a series of categorical variables (see below) that are added together to provide a "total score"; these are also often treated as continuous variables.
- *Dichotomous variables* are those for which there are only two possible outcomes—for example, male or female, true or false, yes or no.
- *Categorical variables* are those for which there are only a few possible outcomes—for example, race/ethnicity, service branch, or rank. In some instances, categorical variables can be placed on a scale from high to low. An example would be a question that asks people how satisfied they were with a training program on a scale of five responses, from very satisfied to completely dissatisfied. These types of categorical variables are sometimes called *ordinal* variables.

Analyzing Continuous Variables

For continuous variables, you are most likely going to be calculating the mean, which is the average response across all unique IDs. For example, one might be interested in the mean duration, in minutes, of a call to a crisis hotline.

Calculating the Mean in Excel

1. In Excel, calculating a mean is straightforward. Simply highlight the cells for which you want the average and choose the "Average" button from the "AutoSum" dropdown menu in the toolbar.

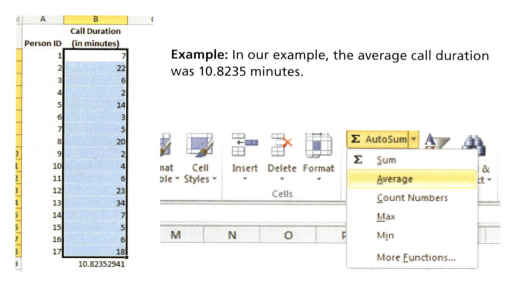

Example: In our example, the average call duration was 10.8235 minutes.

RAND Program Evaluation Toolkit for Countering Violent Extremism

2. When you use the mean, Excel typically includes more values after a decimal point than you might need. To reduce the number of values after the decimal point, choose the applicable cell and click the button indicated below.

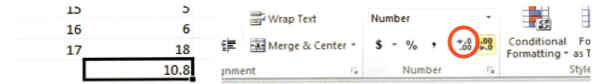

Analyzing Dichotomous Variables

For dichotomous variables, it is almost always the case that you will be calculating a proportion (e.g., the percentage of the sample that completed a particular type of training). For these variables, you simply divide the numerator (e.g., the number of participants who completed the training) by the denominator (e.g., the total number of participants) and multiply by 100 to calculate the percent:

$$\frac{\text{numerator}}{\text{denominator}} \times 100 = \%.$$

Example:

$$\frac{37 \text{ took the training}}{96 \text{ were offered the training}} = 0.385 \times 100 = 38.5\% \text{ of those offered the training completed it.}$$

Calculating Proportions in Microsoft Excel

1. The key to calculating proportions in Microsoft Excel is that when entering the data for each participant, you insert values of 1 for the numerator (e.g., 1 = male) and 0 for everything else (e.g., 0 = female or unspecified)

Example: If you offered a training program to ten people (three women and seven men) and nine completed the training and one did not, your Excel chart would look like this:

	A	B	C
1	Person ID	Sex	Attended training
2	1	0	1
3	2	0	1
4	3	1	1
5	4	0	1
6	5	0	1
7	6	0	1
8	7	1	0
9	8	1	1
10	9	0	1
11	10	0	1

Appendix C: Analyzing Evaluation Data

Note that, in this example, we have coded female as "1" and male as "0." You can assign 1s and 0s to whichever response option you want, but it is critical that you document and are consistent in these assignments.

2. To calculate a proportion, you first need to calculate the total number of individuals in your sample, which will become your denominator. The easiest way to do this in Excel is to use the "Count" command or type, in the case of our example, "=COUNT(A2:A11)" in the cell. Everyone in the sample has an ID (no one has a missing value), so you can ask Excel to count the number of unique IDs.

Example: The first row with a valid ID is A2, and the last row with a valid ID is A11. Thus, in cell A12, we type "=COUNT(A2:A11)," and Excel provides us with the total sample size.

	A	B	C
1	Person ID	Sex	Attended training
2	1	0	1
3	2	0	1
4	3	1	1
5	4	0	1
6	5	0	1
7	6	0	1
8	7	1	0
9	8	1	1
10	9	0	1
11	10	0	1
12	10		

3. Because we have converted our dichotomous variables to 0s and 1s, it is easy to count the total number of women or the total number of participants who completed the training by summing the values in the column. In Excel, the easiest way to do this is to highlight the values in the row and click the "AutoSum" button in the top right corner of the Excel toolbar, or you can type "=SUM(C2:C11)" in the cell. Excel will automatically sum the values in the row and place them in the next available cell in that column (in this case, C12).

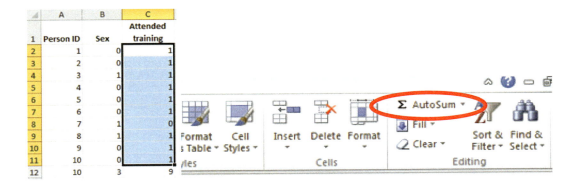

113

4. Now, to calculate the proportion, you divide the numerator (B12) by the denominator (A12). In this example, we chose a cell to display the proportion by typing the following formula in cell D12: (=B12/A12).

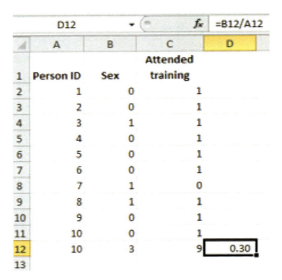

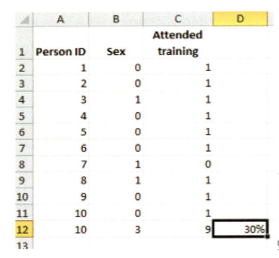

5. If you want to calculate the percentage, simply highlight the cell in which you have just calculated the proportion and click the "%" button on the Excel toolbar.

Analyzing Categorical Variables

For categorical variables, you are most likely going to want to calculate frequencies. This is similar to calculating proportions for dichotomous variables, but for these variables, there are more than two response options. For example, you may want to calculate participants' responses to a questionnaire that asks them to indicate on a five-point scale how likely they are to intervene with someone who is suicidal. For this analysis, you may want to present the proportion reporting to be very likely, somewhat likely, neither likely nor unlikely, somewhat unlikely, or very unlikely. It is important to note that this scale can also be considered an ordinal variable, which, as defined earlier in this primer, is a specific type of categorical variable. Thus, you can assign values to these response options (for example, 5 = very likely, 4 = somewhat likely, 3 = neither likely nor unlikely, 2 = somewhat unlikely, and 1 = very unlikely) and calculate the mean response as if it were a continuous variable.

Calculating Frequencies in Excel

1. To calculate frequencies in Excel, it is easiest to use the "COUNTIF" command. First, make sure your responses are entered into the spreadsheet consistently. If there is any discrepancy (for example, misspelled words, extra spaces, letters that are or are not capitalized), the following strategy will not work. Excel requires the exact same spelling and capitalization to consider responses as part of the same category; these counts are required to determine frequencies for each category.

Example: Your spreadsheet may look like this:

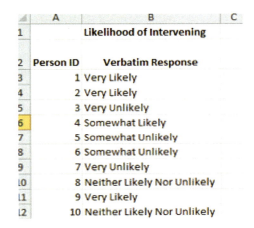

2. Create new cells with all possible response options. In the column next to each, tell Excel to count the number of times within a range of cells a particular response occurs.

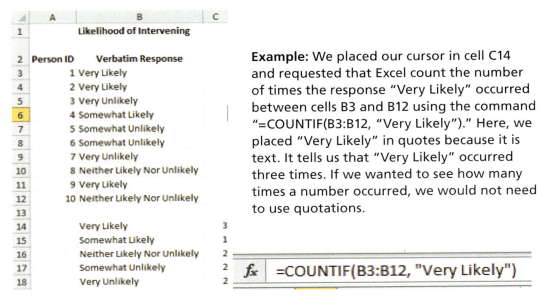

Example: We placed our cursor in cell C14 and requested that Excel count the number of times the response "Very Likely" occurred between cells B3 and B12 using the command "=COUNTIF(B3:B12, "Very Likely")." Here, we placed "Very Likely" in quotes because it is text. It tells us that "Very Likely" occurred three times. If we wanted to see how many times a number occurred, we would not need to use quotations.

RAND Program Evaluation Toolkit for Countering Violent Extremism

3. We can then calculate the proportion as we did earlier for the dichotomous variables. As we mentioned, it might be useful to convert some categorical values into numbers and calculate a mean.

Example: First, we create a new column called "Numeric Response." For each cell, we tell Excel that if the value in the column next to it is "Very Likely," assign a 5; "Somewhat Likely," assign a 4, and so on. This is a somewhat complicated formula that looks like this for each cell in our example:

=IF(B3="Very Likely",5,IF(B3="Somewhat Likely",4,IF(B3="Neither Likely Nor Unlikely",3,IF(B3="Somewhat Unlikely",2,IF(B3="Very Unlikely",1))))).

	A	B	C	D
1		Likelihood of Intervening		
2	Person ID	Verbatim Response		Numeric Response
3	1	Very Likely		5
4	2	Very Likely		5
5	3	Very Unlikely		1
6	4	Somewhat Likely		4
7	5	Somewhat Unlikely		2
8	6	Somewhat Unlikely		2
9	7	Very Unlikely		1
10	8	Neither Likely Nor Unlikely		3
11	9	Very Likely		5
12	10	Neither Likely Nor Unlikely		3

fx =IF(B3="Very Likely",5,IF(B3="Somewhat Likely",4,IF(B3="Neither Likely Nor Unlikely",3,IF(B3="Somewhat Unlikely",2,IF(B3="Very Unlikely",1))))

Once we do this for each cell, we can calculate the mean as if it were a continuous variable:

	A	B	C	D
1		Likelihood of Intervening		
2	Person ID	Verbatim Response		Numeric Response
3	1	Very Likely		5
4	2	Very Likely		5
5	3	Very Unlikely		1
6	4	Somewhat Likely		4
7	5	Somewhat Unlikely		2
8	6	Somewhat Unlikely		2
9	7	Very Unlikely		1
10	8	Neither Likely Nor Unlikely		3
11	9	Very Likely		5
12	10	Neither Likely Nor Unlikely		3
13		Mean		3.10

116

Appendix C: Analyzing Evaluation Data

Summary

Users interested in calculating descriptive statistics may find it useful to abide by the following guidance. First, determine whether your variables are continuous, dichotomous, or categorical.

- If continuous, calculate a mean.
- If dichotomous, calculate a proportion.
- If categorical, calculate frequencies. If ordinal, consider calculating a mean.

RAND Program Evaluation Toolkit for Countering Violent Extremism

Primer 2: Statistical Models for Detecting Differences in Your Program's Target Population

In **Primer 1**, we identified different types of variables: continuous, dichotomous, and categorical. Here, we present guidance on how to detect differences across these variables. Differences may be analyzed by group (for example, those who did or did not receive training) or for individuals (for example, a participant's responses before and after training).

Continuous Variables: Differences in Means

When the goal is to detect how two groups differ for a continuous outcome, you will first need to ensure that the values that you want to compare for each group are normally distributed, which essentially means that they take the shape of a bell curve when their frequencies are plotted in a histogram (shown below).

Examining Whether a Variable Is Normally Distributed in Excel

1. To begin, we need to create our data.

Example: In this example, we will look at the distribution of the number of CVE-focused after-school activities that students in a certain group have attended. On the next page, we have a data set of 42 students (column A) and the number of after-school events they completed, which range from one to ten courses (column B). Ignore column C for now.

2. Next, we create column C, which adds the categories in which we want to display the data.

Example: In the example at on the following page, we indicate that we want to categorize data as every single number of after-school events attended, between one and ten. We could have easily grouped the data (e.g., one to three courses, four to six courses, seven to ten courses), especially if we were looking at data with more than ten discrete outcomes.

3. To plot a histogram of our data, first click the "Data Analysis" button.

4. Highlight the "Histogram" option and click "OK." You will need to specify your input range and bin range (see example below).

Example: Using the data from the example table, in the input range box, either type "B2:B43," or highlight the cells with the numeric values in the second column. In the bin range box, type "C2:C11," or highlight the numeric values in the third column. This second column tells Excel how we want to group our data.

118

Appendix C: Analyzing Evaluation Data

	A	B	C
1	Personal Identification	CVE After-School Activities	Bins
2	001	2	1
3	002	2	2
4	003	1	3
5	004	10	4
6	005	9	5
7	006	8	6
8	007	7	7
9	008	7	8
10	009	3	9
11	010	3	10
12	011	3	
13	012	4	
14	013	4	
15	014	4	
16	015	4	
17	016	4	
18	017	4	
19	018	3	
20	019	3	
21	020	7	
22	021	1	
23	022	8	
24	023	5	
25	024	4	
26	025	3	
27	026	2	
28	027	6	
29	028	6	
30	029	6	
31	030	6	
32	031	7	
33	032	8	
34	033	6	
35	034	7	
36	035	5	
37	036	5	
38	037	6	
39	038	5	
40	039	5	
41	040	5	
42	041	5	
43	042	6	

Note: Respondents 001–021 are from High Schools 1 and 2, and respondents 022–042 are from High Schools 3 and 4.

5. Make sure the "Chart Output" button option is selected and then click "OK." A new Excel worksheet will be created that you can access using the worksheet tabs in the bottom left of the screen. This new tab will have two pieces of output. The first is a frequency table, which summarizes how many people responded with a specific answer. The second is a histogram, which appears to the right of the table and provides a visual representation of the frequency data.

Example: In the example below, the frequency table (left) shows that seven people responded that they had participated four CVE after-school events. The frequencies are also displayed in the histogram (right).

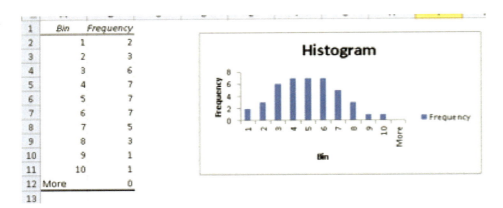

6. To check that the data are normally distributed, we look to see whether there is a bell shape to the histogram. A bell-shaped histogram would tend to show a smaller frequency at the far right and left sides and a greater frequency in the middle. Note that reviewing a histogram is an imprecise way of determining the normality of your data. If possible, working with a statistician to conduct statistical tests is the best way to determine whether your data are normally distributed.

Example: Our histogram has a bell shape. Therefore, we can assume that our data are normally distributed.

7. Are the data normally distributed?

   – *If the variable is normally distributed in both groups:* If, in each of two groups, the variable is normally distributed, you will conduct a student's t-test. You will calculate a t-statistic, which has a corresponding p-value. Again, it is generally accepted that p-values less than 0.05 provide evidence that the two groups differ. Steps for conducting a t-test using Excel are provided on the following page.

   – *If the variable is not normally distributed in both groups:* If the variable is not normally distributed in one or both of the two groups, you will need to conduct a Wilcoxon-Mann-Whitney test. The Wilcoxon-Mann-Whitney test is one of a family of nonparametric statistical tests. Nonparametric tests are based on ranks, rather than raw data, and ranking in Excel is error-prone and not straightforward. In addition, the formulas for these tests are unwieldy, and it is easy to make a mistake. We suggest contacting a statistician or data scientist if you find yourself in need of such a test.

8. Do you have more than two groups to compare?

   – *To compare means of normally distributed variables across more than two groups:* If the variable of interest is normally distributed and you want to compare it across more than two groups, you will conduct a one-way analysis of variance (ANOVA). You will

Appendix C: Analyzing Evaluation Data

calculate an F-statistic, which has a corresponding p-value. *Note that a p-value will tell you only whether one mean is different from another mean; it will not tell you which means (or whether multiple means) differ from each other.* For this process, you will need to calculate t-tests between each pair of groups being compared. Steps for conducting an ANOVA and t-tests using Excel are described below.

— *To compare means of non–normally distributed variables across more than two groups:* If the variable of interest is not normally distributed and you want to compare it across more than two groups, you will conduct a Kruskal-Wallis test. Here, you calculate a chi-square test statistic, which, as mentioned earlier, has associated degrees of freedom and p-value. *Note that a p-value will tell you only whether one mean is different from another mean; it will not tell you which means (or whether multiple means) differ from each other.* For this process, you will need to calculate student's t-tests between each of the two groups being compared. Steps for conducting a chi-square test are presented in **Primer 1**. Steps for conducting a t-test using Excel are below.

Conducting a T-Test in Excel

1. To conduct a t-test, click the "Data Analysis" button.
2. Highlight the "T-Test: Two-Sample Assuming Unequal Variances" option and click "OK."
3. You will need to specify your input range and variable 2 range (see example below). Then click "OK."

Example: Using the previous example involving the number of after-school activities attended, respondents 001–020 are participants from High Schools 1 and 2, and respondents 021–042 are from High Schools 3 and 4. To compare these two groups (High School 1 and High School 2 versus High School 3 and High School 4), in the input range box, either type "A2:A22" or highlight the cells and hit "Enter." For the variable 2 range cell, either type "A23:A43" or highlight the cells and hit "Enter."

4. A new tab will be added to the current tabs at the bottom left of the screen. This new tab will have the t-test output.

5. We can then use the p-value to infer whether the findings are significant.

Conducting an ANOVA in Excel

1. To conduct an ANOVA, first click the "Data Analysis" button.
2. Highlight the "ANOVA: Single Factor" option and click "OK."
3. You will need to specify your input range (see example). Then click "OK."

RAND Program Evaluation Toolkit for Countering Violent Extremism

Example: Using the previous example involving the number of after-school activities attended, respondents 001–021 are from High Schools 1 and 2, and respondents 022–042 are from High Schools 3 and 4. To compare these four groups (1, 2, 3, and 4), you first need to calculate the means for each group. See **Primer 1** for instructions on calculating means. In the input range box, either type "B2:E2" or highlight the cells.

	High School 1	High School 2	High School 3	High School 4
Mean number of after-school activities attended	5.2	4.0	4.7	5.833333333

4. A new tab will be added to the present tabs at the bottom left of the screen. This new tab will have the ANOVA output. Under "F" in the lower table is the F-statistic.

Example: The F-statistic in the previous example is 0.614. The p-value for this example is 0.641. Because the p-value is above 0.05, we cannot infer that the means of the various ranking groups are different from one another.

Dichotomous Variables: Differences in Proportions

When the goal is to detect differences in proportions, a common method is a chi-square test. Below, we summarize the steps to conduct a chi-square test. Steps 1–8 explain how to calculate chi-square for two groups. In our example, we used youth (15–18 years old) participating in a CVE-focused after-school program at High-School 1 versus High-School 2. If you have more than two groups (e.g., additional youth from High-Schools 3 and 4) skip to Step 9. The ability to use this method depends on how many people you are studying.

Calculating Chi-Square in Excel

1. The first step is to create what is known as a *contingency table*. For dichotomous variables, this is a 2×2 table. It is important to note that the procedure we describe here does not work when one of the A, B, C, or D cells has five or fewer individuals. Although there are statistical procedures for handling the scenario of five or fewer individuals in a cell, we suggest consulting with a statistician.

Example: You may want to compare how many participants from High School 1 versus participants from High School 2 who were invited to participate in the after-school program actually participated:

Variable	High School 1	High School 2
Participated in after-school program	A	B
Did not participate	C	D

Appendix C: Analyzing Evaluation Data

2. You must have at least five observations in each cell above (A, B, C, and D) to continue. If you have fewer than five observations in one or more cells, your results will be biased. In this case, you need to perform a different test, which will require the assistance of a statistician. When you have at least five observations in each of the cells (A, B, C, and D), you can conduct a *chi-square test*. Here, you will calculate what is called a *chi-square test statistic*. For each chi-square test statistic, there are two corresponding values: the degree of freedom and the p-value. For a 2×2 table, there will always be one degree of freedom. The p-value is used to indicate whether there is evidence that the two groups are different. It is generally accepted that p-values less than 0.05 indicate that the two groups differ.

3. To determine the chi-square statistic, we begin filling in the numbers in each of the cells (A, B, C, D) of the contingency table.

4. Then, we calculate subtotals across the rows and columns in the table using the "Auto-Sum" function. To do this, highlight the numbers you want to sum and then click the "AutoSum" button, or you can type "=SUM: (B2:C2)" into cell D2 to get the row 2 subtotal, for example.

	A	B	C
1	Observed	High School 1	High School 2
2	Participated in after-school program	20	10
3	Did not participate	30	5

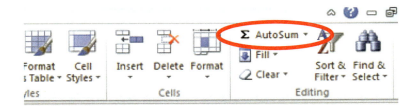

5. Repeat this process until all the subtotals are filled in.

	A	B	C	D
1	Observed	High School 1	High School 2	Subtotal
2	Participated in after-school program	20	10	30
3	Did not participate	30	5	35
4	Subtotal			

RAND Program Evaluation Toolkit for Countering Violent Extremism

6. Next, we need to create another table. We use the totals in the original table to specify the number of "expected" outcomes in each cell. This new table becomes a hypothetical comparison group that will allow us to assess whether there was a difference between participants from High School 1 and High School 2. To do this, we enter the expected value into each cell in the new 2×2 table (excluding the subtotal cell). The expected value for a given cell is defined as

$$\frac{\text{row total} \times \text{column total}}{\text{table total}}.$$

Example: To calculate the expected value for the number of individuals from High School 1 who participated in the training (G2), in our new table, we type the formula "=(D2*B4)/D4"—which, in this case, is (30*50)/65. In this example, the row total is 30 (D2), the column total is 50 (B4), and the table total is 65 (D4). Repeat this process until all four cells are filled and look like the table on the right.

	A	B	C	D	E	F	G	H
1	Observed	High School 1	High School 2	Subtotal		Expected	High School 1	High School 2
2	Participated in after-school program	20	10	30		Participated in after-school program	23.08	6.92
3	Did not participate	30	5	35		Did not participate	26.92	8.08
4	Subtotal							

7. Next, we calculate the p-value based on the chi-square test. Click in a blank cell and type "=CHISQ.TEST(B2:C3,G2:H3)." Note that B2:C3 is the range of values in the original table, and G2:H3 is the range of values in the expected table. These numbers will differ if your tables are in different cells.

8. The p-value returned for this equation is 0.06921. Because this number is greater than 0.05, we can infer that we do not have evidence that these groups differ with respect to whether they took the training.

9. Do you have more than two groups to compare?

    The procedure for performing a chi-square test across more than two groups is very similar to the one described in our earlier example. This time, however, we examine our data divided among a few more categories.

10. To determine whether there is a difference between various groups' tendency to attend a given training, we first create a table of our observed results (shown below). Once again, we will have to calculate the row and column subtotals, as well as the overall total.

11. We then create the expected outcomes to use as a comparison group. We do this for all cells.

Appendix C: Analyzing Evaluation Data

Example: To calculate the expected value for the High School 1 group that took the training, we choose a cell to display the formula and type "=(F2*B4)/F4."

12. Finally, calculate the p-value for the observed data. To do this, click in a blank cell and type "=CHISQ.TEST(B2:E3,I2:L3)." Again, the cell numbers in this formula will differ if your tables use different cells.

Example: The p-value returned for this equation is 0.01265. Because this number is less than 0.05, we can infer that these groups do differ with respect to whether they took the training.

	A	B	C	D	E	F	G	H	I	J	K	L
1	Observed	High School 1	High School 2	High School 3	High School 4	Subtotal		Expected	High School 1	High School 2	High School 3	High School 4
2	Participated in after-school program	10	15	30	25	80		Participated in after-school program	13.79	19.31	22.07	24.83
3	Did not participate	15	20	10	20	65		Did not participate	11.21	15.69	17.93	20.17
4	Subtotal	25	35	40	45	145						
5												
6												
7					p-value	0.0126579						

13. Note that when using more than one group, this process does not tell us specifically which groups differ from which. For this, we will need to run a series of tests using 2×2 tables to indicate which group differs from the others. Unfortunately, we need to run a test for every possible pairing.

Example: In our example, there are six possible pairings: High School 1 versus High School 2, High School 1 versus High School 3, High School 1 versus High School 4, High School 2 versus High School 3, High School 2 versus High School 4, and High School 3 versus High School 4). After conducting each of these six tests, we see evidence that there are differences in attendance between High School 3 and High School 1 (p-value = 0.03), between High School 2 and High School 3 (p-value = 0.01), and between High School 3 and High School 4 (p-value = 0.03). We can thus conclude that participants from High School 3, of whom 75 percent took the training, were more likely to take the training than students in High School 1 (of whom 40 percent took the training), High School 2 (of whom 43 percent took the training), and High School 4 (of whom 56 percent took the training). Steps for calculating percentages are described in **Primer 1**.

125

RAND Program Evaluation Toolkit for Countering Violent Extremism

Categorical Variables: Differences in Frequencies

1. You can still use the chi-square tests described here to test differences in frequencies (for example, the proportion of students who were very likely, somewhat likely, neither likely nor unlikely, somewhat unlikely, or very unlikely to ask for help before and after participating in the after-school program).
2. In this case, you create an R×C contingency table, where R stands for "row" and C stands for "column."

Example: You may want to test whether participants from different high schools reported different coping strategies:

Time Frame	Very Likely	Somewhat Likely	Neither Likely nor Unlikely	Somewhat Unlikely	Very Unlikely
Before participating in after-school program	A	B	C	D	E
After participating in after-school program	F	G	H	I	J
Did not participate	K	L	M	N	O

3. It is important to note that, in this case, the test will only tell you whether one proportion is different from another proportion; it will not tell you which proportions (or whether multiple proportions) differ from each other. For this process, you will need to calculate chi-square tests between each of the two groups being compared. Steps for calculating chi-square tests are provided in **Primer 1**.

126

Appendix C: Analyzing Evaluation Data

Primer 3: Linking Process to Outcome Measures

In this statistical primer, we describe some ways to measure associations between variables, which will enable us to test whether such variables as dosage/attendance, satisfaction, and fidelity are associated with program outcomes.

Both Variables Are Dichotomous

1. When the goal is to detect whether one dichotomous variable is associated with another, you will use the same rule as you did for testing differences in proportions in **Primer 2**. The first step is to create a 2×2 table.

Example: You may want to compare whether those who participated in the CVE-based after-school program were more likely to intervene on behalf of a person in crisis than were those who did not take the training:

Variable	Intervened	Did Not Intervene
Took program	A	B
Did not attend program	C	D

2. In essence, you are still testing the difference in proportions: whether the proportion of those who intervened was larger among those who took the training than among those who did not take the training. That is,

$$\frac{A}{A+B} > \frac{C}{C+D}.$$

3. Recall from **Primer 2** that when the number in each cell is larger than 5, you will conduct a chi-square test. See **Primer 2** for instructions for conducting this test in Excel. You must have at least five observations in each cell above (A, B, C, and D) to continue. If you have fewer than five observations in one or more cells, your results will be biased. In this case, you need to perform a different test, which will require the assistance of a statistician.

Both Variables Are Continuous

1. In certain cases, you may want to examine how two continuous variables are related. In statistical terminology, we use estimates of correlation to quantify the relationship between two continuous variables.

Example: You might measure satisfaction with a training session on a scale from 1 to 100, and you might measure an outcome as symptoms on a scale from 1 to 50.

RAND Program Evaluation Toolkit for Countering Violent Extremism

2. In this case, as shown in **Primer 2**, you will first need to ensure that the values that you want to compare among each group are *normally distributed*, which essentially means that they take the shape of a bell curve when their frequencies are plotted in a histogram.

3. Are variables normally distributed?

    – *When both variables are normally distributed*, you will calculate the Pearson correlation coefficient (often indicated as r). When r is greater than 0, this indicates that the two variables are positively correlated (as one increases, the other increases). If r is less than 0, then the two variables are negatively correlated (as one increases, the other decreases). Finally, if r is equal to 0, the two variables are uncorrelated: There is no linear relationship between them. Like the test statistics we calculated in **Primer 2**, r also has a p-value. It is generally accepted that p-values less than 0.05 provide evidence that the two variables are significantly correlated (either negatively or positively).

    – *When one or both variables are not normally distributed*, you can still assess whether they are associated with each other. In this case, you will calculate the Spearman rank-correlation coefficient (often indicated as r_s). You can interpret r_s in the same way that you interpreted r above. When you have ten or more observations, r_s also has a p-value. It is generally accepted that p-values less than 0.05 provide evidence that two variables are significantly correlated (either negatively or positively).

Calculating the Pearson Correlation Coefficient in Excel

1. To calculate the Pearson correlation coefficient in Excel, we first need to obtain or enter the raw data.

	A	B
	Intervened	Participated in Program
1		
2	1	1
3	1	1
4	0	1
5	1	0
6	0	1
7	1	1
8	0	1
9	1	1
10	0	0
11	1	1
12	1	1
13	1	1
14	1	1
15	1	1
16	1	1

Example: We will create a list of observations for whether an individual intervened on behalf of a person in crisis and whether or not the intervening individual took the training. The two variables, which we label "intervened" and "took training," are called dichotomous variables, because they can have only two outcomes: yes (1) or no (0).

128

Appendix C: Analyzing Evaluation Data

2. Now that the data are entered, in the data toolbar ribbon, click the "Data Analysis" button.

3. In the "Analysis Tools" list, highlight "Correlation" and click "OK."

4. In the next window, in the input range box, either drag and hold the cursor over all the numeric data or enter "A2:B16" in the box. Make sure that "Group by Columns" is selected and click "OK."

5. A new Excel tab is created and, in this case, a 2×2 cell output table is also created. The output table shows the correlation coefficient between the two variables in our raw data.

	A	B	C
1		Column 1	Column 2
2	Column 1	1	
3	Column 2	0.206959	1

6. Column 1 × column 1 and column 2 × column 2, by definition, should always equal 1. This means the two columns are perfectly correlated.

Example: We are interested in the column 1 x column 2 output. A strong correlation is close to 1, and a weak correlation is close to 0. The result is 0.207, which means that the two columns are weakly correlated.

Both Variables Are Categorical

When both variables are ordinal: In **Primer 1**, we explained that categorical variables are sometimes *ordinal*. If you have two ordinal variables (for example, satisfaction with a course on a scale from 1 to 5 and the number of training sessions a person attended), you can examine whether they are correlated using the Spearman rank-correlation coefficient, described earlier.

When neither variable is ordinal: To examine how two categorical variables are associated with each other when neither is ordinal, you can still use the chi-square to determine whether there are differences in proportions, described in **Primer 2**.

One Variable Is Dichotomous, and One Is Continuous

If you have one dichotomous variable (for example, did or did not intervene) and you are interested in whether it is associated with a continuous variable (for example, performance, measured on a scale from 1 to 100), you can use the methods for comparing means across two groups (student's t-test, Wilcoxon-Mann-Whitney test) described in **Primer 2**.

One Variable Is Categorical, and One Is Dichotomous

If you have one dichotomous variable (for example, did or did not intervene) and you are interested in whether it is associated with a categorical variable (for example, satisfaction, measured on a scale from 1 to 5), you can use the methods for comparing proportions across more than two groups (chi-square test) described in **Primer 2**.

RAND Program Evaluation Toolkit for Countering Violent Extremism

One Variable Is Categorical, and One Is Continuous

If you have one categorical variable (for example, satisfaction measured on a scale from 1 to 5) and you are interested in whether it is associated with a continuous variable (for example, performance, measured on a scale from 1 to 100), you can use the methods for comparing means across more than two groups (ANOVA or Kruskal-Wallis test) described in **Primer 2**.

Summary

Nice job completing your evaluation data analysis! This appendix provided information about how you can get support to analyze data (e.g., through a statistical software package or through an evaluation or statistics expert) and included three primers to support some basic data analysis using Microsoft Excel. After using this appendix, you should have selected your evaluation data analysis strategy and begun implementing it—whether on your own or with help from the experts.

Glossary of Terms

Evidence-based program
A program that has been determined to be effective through rigorous scientific evaluations and randomized controlled trials, has a significant and sustained effect on intended outcomes, and has been tested using large longitudinal studies or multiple replications (Evidence-Based Prevention and Intervention Support Center, undated).

Fidelity
Adherence of implementation to a program's original design (Smith, Daunic, and Taylor, 2007).

Logic model
A graphical depiction of the rationale and expectations of a program (Leviton et al., 2010). A logic model clarifies the causal relationships among program resources, activities, and outcomes (McLaughlin and Jordan, 1999; Wholey, Hatry, and Newcomer, 2010).

Outcomes
Changes or benefits resulting from activities and outputs. Typically, programs have short-, intermediate-, and long-term outcomes (Leviton et al., 2010; Wholey, Hatry, and Newcomer, 2010).

Outcome evaluation
An assessment of the extent to which the program's activities or services have brought about expected changes in the target population or social condition (Rossi, Lipsey, and Freeman, 2004).

Outputs
The products, goods, and services provided to the program's participants (Wholey, Hatry, and Newcomer, 2010).

Process evaluation
A form of program evaluation designed to document and analyze the early development and actual implementation of a program, assessing whether and how well services are delivered as intended or planned. Also known as implementation assessment (Wholey, Hatry, and Newcomer, 2010; Rossi, Lipsey, and Freeman, 2004).

Program
A set of activities, tied together through shared resources (e.g., staff, funding, space, materials), meant to influence a target population's knowledge, attitudes, or behavior to accomplish a specific goal or goals.

References

Acosta, Joie, and Matthew Chinman, "Building Capacity for Outcomes Measurement in Human Service Organizations: The Getting To Outcomes Method," in Jennifer L. Magnabosco and Ronald W. Manderscheid, eds., *Outcomes Measurement in the Human Services: Cross-Cutting Issues and Methods in the Era of Health Reform*, Washington, D.C.: NASW Press, 2011.

Acosta, Joie, Rajeev Ramchand, Amariah Becker, Alexandra Felton, and Aaron Kofner, *RAND Suicide Prevention Program Evaluation Toolkit*, Santa Monica, Calif.: RAND Corporation, TL-111-OSD, 2013. As of January 17, 2017:
http://www.rand.org/pubs/tools/TL111.html

American Evaluation Association, "Find an Evaluator," web page, undated. As of November 25, 2016:
http://www.eval.org/p/cm/ld/fid=108

Amjad, Naumana, and Alex M. Wood, "Identity and Changing the Normative Beliefs About Aggression Which Lead Young Muslim Adults to Join Extremist Anti-Semitic Groups in Pakistan," *Aggressive Behavior*, Vol. 35, No. 6, November–December 2009, pp. 514–519.

Bandura, Albert, "Guide for Constructing Self-Efficacy Scales," in Frank Pajares and Tim Urdan, eds., *Self-Efficacy Beliefs of Adolescents*, Charlotte, N.C.: Information Age Publishing, 2006.

Barkman, Susan J., *A Field Guide to Designing Quantitative Instruments to Measure Program Impact*, West Lafayette, Ind.: Purdue University, 2002.

Beaghley, Sina, Todd C. Helmus, Miriam Matthews, Rajeev Ramchand, David Stebbins, Amanda Kadlec, and Michael A. Brown, *Development and Pilot Test of the RAND Program Evaluation Toolkit for Countering Violent Extremism*, Santa Monica, Calif.: RAND Corporation, RR-1799-DHS, 2017. As of February 2017:
http://www.rand.org/pubs/research_reports/RR1799.html

Beck, Aaron T., Norman Epstein, Gary Brown, and Robert A. Steer, "An Inventory for Measuring Clinical Anxiety: Psychometric Properties," *Journal of Consulting and Clinical Psychology*, Vol. 56, No. 6, December 1988, pp. 893–897.

Belmont Report—*See* National Commission for the Protection of Human Subjects of Biomedical and Behavioral Research.

Berk, Ronald, Janet Berg, Rosemary Mortimer, Benita Walton-Moss, and Theresa P. Yep, "Measuring the Effectiveness of Faculty Mentoring Relationships," *Academic Medicine*, Vol. 80, No. 1, January 2005, pp. 66–71.

Bobek, Deborah, Jonathan Zaff, Yibing Li, and Richard M. Lerner, "Cognitive, Emotional, and Behavioral Components of Civic Action: Towards an Integrated Measure of Civic Engagement," *Journal of Applied Developmental Psychology*, Vol. 30, No. 5, September–October 2009, pp. 615–627.

Broadhead, W. E., Stephan Gehlbach, Frank V. DeGruy, and Berton H. Kaplan, "The Duke-UNC Functional Support Questionnaire: Measurement of Social Support in Family Medicine Patients," *Medical Care*, Vol. 26, No. 7, July 1988, pp. 709–723.

Chavez, Christine, *Survey Design*, Los Angeles, Calif.: Loyola Marymount University, 2016.

RAND Program Evaluation Toolkit for Countering Violent Extremism

Chavis, David M., Kien S. Lee, and Joie D. Acosta, "The Sense of Community (SCI) Revised: The Reliability and Validity of the SCI-2," paper presented at the 2nd International Community Psychology Conference, Lisbon, Portugal, 2008.

Chinman, Matthew, Joie Acosta, Patricia Ebener, Q. Burkhart, Michael Clifford, Maryann Corsello, Tim Duffey, Sarah Hunter, Margaret Jones, Michael Lahti, Patrick S. Malone, Susan Paddock, Andrea Phillips, Susan Savell, Peter C. Scales, and Nancy Tellett-Royce, "Establishing and Evaluating the Key Functions of an Interactive Systems Framework Using an Assets–Getting To Outcomes Intervention," *American Journal of Community Psychology*, Vol. 350, Nos. 3–4, December 2012, pp. 295–310.

———, "Intervening with Practitioners to Improve the Quality of Prevention: One Year Findings from a Randomized Trial of Assets–Getting To Outcomes," *Journal of Primary Prevention*, Vol. 34, No. 3, June 2013, pp. 173–191.

Code of Federal Regulations, Title 45, Part 46, Protection of Human Subjects (Common Rule), effective July 14, 2009. As of January 17, 2017:
http://www.hhs.gov/ohrp/regulations-and-policy/regulations/45-cfr-46/index.html

Crano, William, and Marilynn B. Brewer, *Principles and Methods of Social Research*, 2nd ed., Mahwah, N.J.: Lawrence Erlbaum Associates, 2002.

Crow, David, and Robert Luskin, *Citizen Disenchantment in Mexico (national survey, June 2006)*, Ann Arbor, Mich.: Inter-University Consortium for Political and Social Research, August 2013.

Cummins, Robert A., Marta P. McCabe, Yolanda Romeo, and Eleonora Gullone, "The Comprehensive Quality of Life Scale (ComQol): Instrument Development and Psychometric Evaluation on College Staff and Students," *Educational and Psychological Measurement*, Vol. 54, No. 2, Summer 1994, pp. 372–382.

Cutrona, Carolyn E., and Daniel W. Russell, "The Provisions of Social Relationships and Adaptation to Stress," *Advances in Personal Relationships*, Vol. 1, 1987, pp. 37–67.

DeVellis, Robert F., *Scale Development: Theory and Applications*, 3rd ed., Washington D.C.: Sage Publications, 2012.

Diem, Keith, *A Step-by-Step Guide to Developing Effective Questionnaires and Survey Procedures for Program Evaluation and Research*, New Brunswick, N.J.: Rutgers University, 2002.

Dillman, Don A., Jolene D. Smyth, and Leah Melani Christina, *Internet, Mail, and Mixed-Mode Surveys: The Tailored Design Method*, 3rd ed., New York: John Wiley and Sons, 2009.

Dowler, Kenneth, and Valerie Zawilski, "Public Perceptions of Police Misconduct and Discrimination: Examining the Impact of Media Consumption," *Journal of Criminal Justice*, Vol. 35, No. 2, March–April 2007, pp. 193–203.

Evidence-Based Prevention and Intervention Support Center, "Defining Evidence Based Programs," web page, undated. As of January 17, 2017:
http://www.episcenter.psu.edu/ebp/definition

Executive Office of the President, *Strategic Implementation Plan for Empowering Local Partners to Prevent Violent Extremism in the United States*, Washington, D.C.: White House, October 2016.

Henry, P. J., and David O. Sears, "The Symbolic Racism 2000 Scale," *Political Psychology*, Vol. 23, No. 2, June 2002, pp. 253–283.

Hunter, Sarah B., Patricia A. Ebener, Matthew Chinman, Allison J. Ober, and Christina Y. Huang, *Promoting Success: A Getting To Outcomes® Guide to Implementing Continuous Quality Improvement for Community Service Organizations*, Santa Monica, Calif.: RAND Corporation, TL-179-NIDA, 2015. As of January 17, 2017:
http://www.rand.org/pubs/tools/TL179.html

Kaplan, Andreas M., and Michael Haenlein, "Users of the World, Unite! The Challenges and Opportunities of Social Media," *Business Horizons*, Vol. 53, No. 1, January–February 2010, pp. 59–68.

Kapp, Julie M., Colleen Peters, and Debra Parker Oliver, "Research Recruitment Using Facebook Advertising: Big Potential, Big Challenges," *Journal of Cancer Education*, Vol. 28, No. 1, March 2013, pp. 134–137.

References

Katz, Irwin, and R. Glen Hass, "Racial Ambivalence and American Value Conflict: Correlational and Priming Studies of Dual Cognitive Structures," *Journal of Personality and Social Psychology*, Vol. 55, No. 6, December 1988, pp. 893–905.

Kettner, Peter M., Robert M. Moroney, and Lawrence L. Martin, *Designing and Managing Programs: An Effectiveness-Based Approach*, 4th ed., Washington D.C.: Sage Publications, 2013.

Kinder, Donald R., and D. Roderick Kiewiet, "Economic Discontent and Political Behavior: The Role of Personal Grievances and Collective Economic Judgments in Congressional Voting," *American Journal of Political Science*, Vol. 23, No. 3, August 1979, pp. 495–527.

LaFree, Gary, Stanley Presser, Roger Tourangeau, and Amy Adamczyk, *U.S. Attitudes Toward Terrorism and Counterterrorism: Report to the U.S. Department of Homeland Security, Science and Technology Directorate's Resilient Systems Division*, College Park, Md.: National Consortium for the Study of Terrorism and Responses to Terrorism, 2013.

LaMotte, Valerie, Kelly Ouellette, Jessica Sanderson, Stephen A. Anderson, Iva Kosutic, Julie Griggs, and Marison Garcia, "Effective Police Interactions with Youth," *Police Quarterly*, Vol. 13, No. 2, 2010, pp. 161–179.

Lesesne, C. A., K. M. Lewis, C. Moore, D. Fisher, D. Green, and A. Wandersman, *Promoting Science-Based Approaches to Teen Pregnancy Prevention Using Getting to Outcomes: Draft 2011*, unpublished manual, 2011.

Leviton, Laura C., Laura Kettel Khan, Debra Rog, Nicola Dawkins, and David Cotton, "Evaluability Assessment to Improve Public Health Policies, Programs, and Practices," *Annual Review of Public Health*, Vol. 31, 2010, pp. 213–233.

Lillis, Jason, and Steven C. Hayes, "Applying Acceptance, Mindfulness, and Values to the Reduction of Prejudice: A Pilot Study," *Behavior Modification*, Vol. 31, No. 4, July 2007, pp. 389–411.

McLaughlin, John A., and Gretchen B. Jordan, "Logic Models: A Tool for Telling Your Program's Performance Story," *Evaluation and Program Planning*, Vol. 22, No. 1, February 1999, pp. 65–72.

National Commission for the Protection of Human Subjects of Biomedical and Behavioral Research, *The Belmont Report*, Washington, D.C.: U.S. Department of Health, Education, and Welfare, 1979. As of January 17, 2017:
http://www.hhs.gov/ohrp/regulations-and-policy/belmont-report/index.html

Omoto, Allen M., Mark Snyder, and Justin D. Hackett, "Personality and Motivational Antecedents of Activism and Civic Engagement," *Journal of Personality*, Vol. 78, No. 6, December 2010, pp. 1703–1734.

Pew Research Center, *Muslim Americans: No Signs of Growth in Alienation or Support for Extremism*, Washington, D.C., 2011.

Plant, E. Ashby, and Patricia G. Devine, "Internal and External Motivation to Respond Without Prejudice," *Journal of Personality and Social Psychology*, Vol. 75, No. 3, September 1998, pp. 811–832.

Poister, Theodore H., "Performance Measurement: Monitoring Program Outcomes," in Joseph S. Wholey, Harry P. Hatry, and Kathryn E. Newcomer, eds., *Handbook of Practical Program Evaluation*, 3rd ed., San Francisco, Calif.: Jossey-Bass, 2010, pp. 100–124.

Rew, Lynn, Heatehr Becker, Jeff Cookston, Shirin Khosropour, and Stephanie Martinez, "Measuring Cultural Awareness in Nursing Students," *Journal of Nursing Education*, Vol. 42, No. 6, June 2003, pp. 249–257.

RAND Corporation, "Getting To Outcomes®: Improving Community-Based Prevention," web page, undated. As of January 17, 2017:
http://www.rand.org/health/projects/getting-to-outcomes.html

Rocha, Cynthia J., "Evaluating Experiential Teaching Methods in a Policy Practice Course: The Case for Service Learning to Increase Political Participation," *Higher Education*, Paper 64, 2000.

Rossi, Peter H., Mark W. Lipsey, and Howard E. Freeman, *Evaluation: A Systematic Approach*, 7th ed., Thousand Oaks, Calif.: Sage Publications, 2004.

Salant, Priscilla, and Don A. Dillman, *How to Conduct Your Own Survey*, New York: John Wiley and Sons, 1994.

Sarason, Irwin G., Henry M. Evine, Robert B. Basham, and Barbara R. Sarason, "Assessing Social Support: The Social Support Questionnaire," *Journal of Personality and Social Psychology*, Vol. 44, No. 1, January 1983, pp. 127–139.

Schaefer, Joseph A., Beth M. Huebner, and Timothy S. Bynum, "Citizen Perceptions of Police Services: Race, Neighborhood Context, and Community Policing," *Police Quarterly*, Vol. 6, No. 4, December 2003, pp. 440–468.

Smith, Stephen W., Ann P. Daunic, and Gregory G. Taylor, "Treatment Fidelity in Applied Educational Research: Expanding the Adoption and Application of Measures to Ensure Evidence-Based Practice," *Education and Treatment of Children*, Vol. 30, No. 4, November 2007, pp. 121–134.

Snell, William E., Scott Gum, Roger L. Shuck, Jo A. Mosley, and Tamara L. Hite, "The Clinical Anger Scale: Preliminary Reliability and Validity," *Journal of Clinical Psychology*, Vol. 51, No. 2, March 1995, pp. 215–226.

Sweikhart, Mark, Brenda Sinclair, and Refaat Shafeek, *Joint Lessons Learned Assessment of the Basic Education Support and Training (BEST) Project*, Washington, D.C.: U.S. Agency for International Development, 2010. As of January 17, 2017:
http://pdf.usaid.gov/pdf_docs/pnadz876.pdf

Tausch, Nicole, Julia C. Becker, Russell Spears, Oliver Christ, Rim Saab, Purnima Singh, and Roomana N. Siddiqui, "Explaining Radical Group Behavior: Developing Emotion and Efficacy Routes to Normative and Non-Normative Collective Action," *Journal of Personality and Social Psychology*, Vol. 101, No. 1, July 2011, pp. 129–148.

U.S. Agency for International Development, *Mid-Term Evaluation of USAID's Counter-Extremism Programming in Africa*, Washington, D.C., 2011.

USAID—*See* U.S. Agency for International Development.

Van Dam, Nicholas T., and Mitch Earleywine, "Validation of the Center for Epidemiologic Studies Depression Scale–Revised (CESD-R): Pragmatic Depression Assessment in the General Population," *Psychiatry Research*, Vol. 186, No. 1, March 2011, pp. 128–132.

Van Horn, M. Lee, Jeffrey M. Bellis, and Scott W. Snyder, "Family Resource Scale–Revised: Psychometrics and Validation of a Measure of Family Resources in a Sample of Low-Income Families," *Journal of Psychoeducational Assessment*, Vol. 19, No. 1, March 2001, pp. 54–68.

Weatherford, M. Stephen, "Measuring Political Legitimacy," *American Political Science Review*, Vol. 86, No. 1, March 1992, pp. 149–166.

Welch, Eric W., Charles C. Hinnant, and M. Jae Moon, "Linking Citizen Satisfaction with E-Government and Trust in Government," *Journal of Public Administration Research and Theory*, Vol. 15, No. 3, 2005, pp. 371–391.

WhatIs.com, "Search: Blog," web page, undated. As of January 17, 2017:
http://whatis.techtarget.com/search/query?q=blog

Wholey, Joseph S., Harry P. Hatry, and Kathryn E. Newcomer, eds., *Handbook of Practical Program Evaluation*, 3rd ed., New York: John Wiley and Sons, 2010.

Willis, Gordon B., *Cognitive Interviewing: A "How To" Guide, Research Triangle Institute*, short course presented at the 1999 Meeting of the American Statistical Association, 1999.

W. K. Kellogg Foundation, *Logic Model Development Guide*, Battle Creek, Mich.: October 2000.

Zaidise, Eran, Daphne Canetti-Nisim, and Ami Pedahzur, "Politics of God or Politics of Man? The Role of Religion and Deprivation in Predicting Support for Political Violence in Israel," *Political Studies*, Vol. 55, No. 3, October 2007, pp. 499–521.